FROM-

MOLLY,

WITH LOVE

16. 12. 94.

MOLLY   DERRICK

8 QUEENS PK GDNS

BOURNEMOUTH

BH8. 9BN

0202 398230

TROTTING AROUND
IN BRITAIN

Also by Dorothy A. Trott:
Trotting Around, The Book Guild Ltd.

Trotting Around in
BRITAIN

Dorothy A. Trott

The Book Guild Ltd.
Sussex, England

The Book Guild Ltd.
25 High Street.
Lewes, Sussex

First published 1992
© Dorothy A. Trott 1992
Set in Baskerville
Typesetting by Southern Reproductions (Sussex)
East Grinstead, Sussex
Printed in Great Britain by
Antony Rowe Ltd.
Chippenham, Wiltshire

A catalogue record for this book is
available from the British Library

ISBN 0 86332 757 5

CONTENTS

List of Illustrations   6
Acknowledgements   8
Introduction   9

PART ONE

The Lake District and North West   13
Yorkshire   15
North Eastern England   23
Scotland   26
Lancashire   34
Isle of Man   36
Welsh Border Counties and Wales   39
Island of Anglesey   46

PART TWO

Derbyshire and the Peak District   49
The Midlands   57
East Midlands and Lincolnshire   60
The Midlands, Leicestershire
    and Rutland   62
East Anglia   64
The West Midlands   70

PART THREE

The West Country   83
South West England   92
South England   100
    The Isle of Wight   101
    Channel Islands   102
The London Area   112

LIST OF ILLUSTRATIONS

Bootham Bar and Cathedral, York 16
Durham Cathedral 24
Edinburgh Castle 28
The Amis Reunis, Portmeirion, Wales 42
Chesterfield Church 50
Bakewell well dressing 52
Poole, Dorset 89
Clovelly, Devonshire 94
St Michael's Mount 98
Sissinghurst, Kent 108

I travelled among unknown men
In lands beyond the sea;
Nor England did I know till then
What love I bore to thee.

William Wordsworth

Acknowledgements

I wish to thank my friends, Ralph A. Gale for his assistance in research; Malcolm T. Needham for the illustrative photographs, Eunice A. Nation for all the typing and Janet Coates for editing.

INTRODUCTION

My foster father believed that regular holidays were the best investment and, although his salary was a mere pittance compared with today's earnings, we always had two good holidays a year, one in the spring, the other in early autumn, and sometimes at Christmas too. Thus I developed a love of travel at an early age.

PART

1

THE LAKE DISTRICT
AND NORTH WEST

I was probably born in 1903. Some months later I was taken by some charitable organization to a home for unwanted babies in Grange-over-Sands, a quiet resort on Morecombe Bay. There I was adopted by my foster parents and received into their home at Wortley in South Yorkshire where my foster father was then manager of the iron works.

It was some fourteen years later that I visited the Lake District again, whilst staying with my school friend Connie in Bradford. Her parents had a luxurious motor car, rare in those days, and we went to Bowness for a weekend, sailed on Lake Windermere and walked over the surrounding hills in glorious weather.

In the following year I visited Grange-over-Sands with my parents to spend the Christmas holiday at Hazelwood Hydro and explored this attractive area, little knowing that it had any connection with my early days. I found the homes of the poets Wordsworth, Coleridge, Hazlett, De Quincey, Shelley and Charles Lamb fascinating and it inspired a desire for a closer acquaintance with their work.

The Lake District is a beautiful area of mountains and lakes extending over some thirty square miles. Kendal, an attractive border town on the largest lake, was the birthplace of Katherine Parr, the sixth wife of King Henry VIII, who survived him.

From Ambleside, overlooking Lake Windermere, the road runs north to Ullswater which inspired Wordsworth to write his famous poem The Daffodils. Keswick at the head of the Derwent Water, was the haunt of the huntsman John Peel, of the well-known ballad, and also the home of Coleridge and Southey. Many more famous names such as Appleby, Alnwick, Bamburgh and Lancaster testify to the centuries of strife and violence between the Scots and English; they were frequently besieged and burnt by marauding bands from both countries.

The beautiful cathedrals of this area such as Carlisle, Furness Abbey and smaller religious houses such as Cartmel Priory illustrate the immense and widespread ecclesiastical influence of the Middle Ages.

YORKSHIRE

Wortley in South Yorkshire was my home for several years before my foster father moved to Sheffield to develop a new business at his steelworks and then we lived in various suburbs away from the grime and smoke of the city, until I went to boarding school in Buxton in 1916.

The early years of the 1914-18 War brought a change to our quiet suburban existence for on a nearby hill there was a well-known rifle range used to train the Territorial Army. They had a short intensive course in rifle practice, probably suitable for an eye-to-eye encounter with the enemy, but of little use in the trench warfare of World War I.

The smart newly-uniformed young soldiers came and went in their thousands and I shall never forget the departure of a Highland regiment marching to their bagpipes, their tartan kilts swirling as they made their way to the railway station for the first stage of embarkation to France. In the following week they were wiped out by the enemy at the Battle of Mons.

The huge Zeppelin, like a silver cigar in the moonlight, floating down over the railway track near our house, was a sight to be remembered. We had no idea what it was until the bombs began to fall, and it was finally shot down in flames.

15

Bootham Bar and Cathedral, York

16

In the meantime, to avoid the air raids, my friend Connie moved with her parents to Harrogate and her father travelled each day to his woollen mill in Bradford. During my frequent visits to their lovely home on the Stray we took trips into the fascinating country across the plain of York, exploring the ancient historic city and the beautiful variety of villages in the Yorkshire dales.

The romantic Yorkshire Dales stretch from Halifax, Bradford and the industrial city of Leeds in the West Riding, to Middlesborough, Scotch Corner and Richmond to the River Tees on the Durham border, covering an area of nearly seven hundred miles, now designated a national park.

The mountain scenery rises through wild lovely moors, with caves, potholes and waterfalls; very beautiful in the lower ranges with charming villages, many castles, abbeys, churches and mansions of great historical interest.

On one occasion, we were invited to a garden party at the country home of the Princess Royal and her husband Lord Lascelles, Earl of Harewood. They were charming hosts on such a beautiful day, for a memorable visit to Harewood House and grounds.

☆　☆　☆

My foster father often took me to Bridlington, for he was very fond of sea fishing and this was the nearest resort to our home in Sheffield. He hired a rowing boat for about 5/- (25p) per day and we set out with rods, bait, sandwiches and thermos flasks for a day's sport. He taught me how to row and manage the boat, but I was not too keen on baiting the hooks.

Sometimes we had some luck with a shoal of fish but often we hooked a conger eel, almost as long as the boat

17

and difficult to handle, much less to kill. One of my duties was to keep the boat free from rubbish and, seeing a piece of cork apparently serving no purpose, I threw it overboard and at once the boat began to fill with water. It was of course, the bung which I had discarded so lightly and we had to find a substitute pretty quickly. Nothing seemed to fill the hole in the bottom of the boat, but I remember that we finally whittled down a thermos cork as a temporary measure, tied it down with a handkerchief and hoped for the best.

Scarborough was also another favourite resort, though the fishing was not so good there, but as I grew older I preferred it for a holiday, because of the concerts on the Spa; during the summer months there was a good orchestra and talented soloists.

After the war, my friend Hilda and I often stayed with a kindly old lady Mrs Rowlands who was an excellent cook, so we enjoyed a round of golf on the links at Ganton, returning for a sumptuous dinner before the evening concert. By this time I had acquired an Austin 7, a small sturdy car which travelled everywhere without trouble. In those days there were few macadam roads and many dirt tracks and grass lanes.

I had several holidays with other friends at Mrs Rowlands's until the outbreak of World War II in 1939, the chaos of which closed many of these small seaside establishments.

In 1940 my friend Vera rented a charming little bungalow in a small hamlet called Rillington near Malton, for her son was a pupil at a local farm until he was called up for the army. Here I spent much of my holiday in each of the war years and with her family we toured extensively in that area.

Across the flat agricultural country, so different from the hills of Derbyshire, the vista stretched as far as the eye could see, occasionally broken by a large clump of trees denoting a country house or farm lying in a hollow, whilst the larks rose singing from their nests in the peace and calm of an early summer morning.

In contrast, I well remember, snug in bed on New Year's Eve listening to the sound of the wind twanging the ice-clad telephone wires like a harpist, whilst it piled up the snow in deep drifts; there was no air-raid that night.

There is a delightful coastal road between Scarborough and Whitby, a lively old fishing town at the mouth of the River Esk with its picturesque narrow streets and quaint houses: a twenty foot high carved cross was erected to the memory of Caedmon, father of English literature.

On a hill by the sea stand the ruins of the ancient abbey of 657 AD where the noble Abbess Hilda reigned supreme over her little empire. Captain Cook's house in Grape Lane is still extant from 1688.

South of Scarborough is Filey, another well-known seaside resort built on a line of white cliffs extending to Flamborough Head, an interesting area notable for the nesting of its sea birds.

Some years later, after the war, there was a Soroptimist conference in Harrogate at which Yorkshire members welcomed those from overseas and naturally we visited castles, mansions and seaside resorts in Yorkshire with

19

our guests.

Several years passed, until one day the Independent Schools Association instructed me to organize a national conference for our members.

It was essential that this should be a success, for heads of schools in the South of England could not believe that there was any real civilization north of the Thames and I had to prove them wrong. So, with accommodation in first class hotels, a mayoral reception in the town hall, a chamber concert in the famous gardens and a Cabinet Minister as guest speaker, the Yorkshire members tried to change the concept of the north/south divide. We also entertained the Mayor of Bagnères de Luçon, the French Spa I had visited the previous summer.

Yorkshire is the home of many abbeys, castles and cathedrals of former times including Rievaulx, Fountains, perhaps the most beautiful of British monastic buildings, destroyed in the Reformation of Henry VIII, and the ruins of Bolton Abbey on the banks of the River Wharfe.

Howarth Parsonage, the home of the Brontés, is situated in bleak moorlands not far from Ilkley Moor; it is a forbidding, wild area in the best of weather, so no wonder the novelist needed some recreation.

One of my friends owned a very successful Independent school in Saltburn-by-the-Sea which I visited whenever in the vicinity, in my rôle as chairman of the Yorkshire area of the Independent Schools Association.

It is a holiday resort with some fine cliff scenery

In 1920, after the war, my singing master, Guido Delni, visited Sheffield to build up a nucleus of promising pupils in that area but in 1923 he decided to make his headquarters in Bradford and this move necessitated my travelling to and fro for lessons.

At the time I was not earning any money so my father agreed to pay the fees and a subsidy of 5/- (25p) per week for three months, during which I was to find work to finance the trips myself.

Thus I travelled regularly on an excursion train each week and had a few pence left for a tram to finish my journey to the Delni home, in Manningham Lane.

During this period I saw much of Bradford, the centre of the wool and worsted industry and birth place in 1862 of Frederick Delius, the composer, and of my friend Connie who was now married there. But when the three months had expired my work was bringing in £40 a year and I could afford to pay for the lessons myself

Amidst the rural areas of South Yorkshire is the city of Sheffield, built like Rome on seven hills. It is a large industrial city with a cathedral dating from the 14th and 15th centuries, an important university and a world-wide reputation for the manufacture of cutlery, special steels, as well as heavy engineering and coal mining.

From Chatsworth House, in November, 1580, Mary, Queen of Scots, escorted by the Earl of Shrewsbury, reined in her horse on the ridge above Totley and gazed across the valley to the town where she was to be imprisoned in Sheffield Manor Castle for sixteen unhappy years, under the guardianship of the Earl.

From the days of Chaucer, Sheffield's cutlery earned world-wide fame, being produced in many small workshops and household factories which earned it a reputation for smoke, grime and air pollution. In recent years this domestic method of manufacture has been replaced by huge modern factories and mass production. It is rightly said now that a green field can be seen from every point in the city.

Rotherham is on the River Don, which is spanned by an ancient bridge upon which stands the picturesque chapel of Our Lady. It was built in 1483, and after suppression in 1547, had a chequered life, being used as an alms house, a jail and a shop, before being restored in 1924.

The palatial 18th century mansion of Wentworth-Woodhouse with one of the longest frontages in England, is not far away.

NORTH EASTERN
ENGLAND

The most impressive view of Durham is from the viaduct carrying the train north-bound to Scotland across one of its three fine old bridges. On the opposite hill stands the magnificent cathedral, silhouetted on the skyline and dominating the town, which lies in the hollow beneath it. The ancient edifice founded in 999 AD provides also the most important influence over the whole area, most activities being coloured by the clerical hierarchy. It contains the tomb of the Venerable Bede.

It happened that my stepmother's nephew was a Doctor of Theology and we often stayed with Kingsley and Margaret for a couple of nights, en route to Scotland. Their house was fascinating, full to overflowing with books on every conceivable subject, for Kingsley was a real scholar, a world-renowned lecturer and academic and the number of books certainly increased as their children married and left home, when more space became available.

Durham University is ideally situated on another hill near the cathedral in a very pleasant spacious park, incorporating the ancient castle, an area unspoilt as yet, but useful to provide student accommodation in future. It is a scheme which shows great foresight.

Durham Cathedral

The town itself climbs over the hills with its narrow, steep streets and ancient buildings, denoting its historic past.

Neville's Cross, in memory of the battle fought in 1346 stands on the western outskirts of the city.

Newcastle-upon-Tyne, the county town of Northumberland, once a station of the Roman Wall, is the centre of the industrial complex of the North East, Jarrow, Tynemouth and Wallsend being extensions of the shipbuilding industry and the export of coal. Its situation on the river brought great prosperity to the area in past centuries. Now that shipbuilding is in decline, there is much unemployment and distress.

The River Tyne is spanned by three fine bridges and the city itself contains some beautiful Regency buildings: the Guildhall dates from 1658 and the cathedral mostly 'decorated' and 'perpendicular' work is noted for the rare 'Crown' spire, resembling that of St-Giles in Edinburgh. The castle has a restored 12th century keep and there are Roman remains in the university quadrangle and mediaeval buildings of great interest.

Not far away is Hadrian's Roman Wall dating from 120AD and this extends across England to Bowness on the Solway Firth, built as a bastion against the border Scots.

SCOTLAND

In the spring of 1910 my foster father contracted malaria, a disease little known at that time in this country and diagnosis was delayed until it was established that he had been bitten by mosquitoes discovered in a crate of bananas in Nottingham. Consequently, lacking immediate treatment, he became intensely ill and was absent from work for some months.

It was a long hot summer with many weeks of drought so it was decided that I should spend August in Scotland with a family whilst he convalesced in the South of England.

As a result, my mother took me to the McLaren's house in Glasgow for a couple of days, before I accompanied them to the seaside. Mr McLaren was a braw Scot whose language I could not understand, whilst his wife was a tall angular woman with little charm; they had twin daughters of about eighteen, who did not want to bother with a child of seven.

First we saw something of Glasgow, the largest city and seaport in Scotland which has grown rapidly during the last century due to the enterprise of the inhabitants in developing the River Clyde, to establish large docks, engineering works, shipbuilding yards, chemical and textile industries.

The first cathedral of 1125-1136 was built over the

grave of St Mungo and the present very fine building was erected during the 13th century. The famous university was established in 1450, just before the city became a Royal Burgh. Among many places of interest are the splendid art gallery and museum, Provand's Lordship, probably Glasgow's oldest house, built in 1471 as part of the old Hospital of St Nicholas; it is said that Mary, Queen of Scots lived there in 1566: it's neighbour Provan Hall, of the 15th Century is now Scottish National Trust property.

We also visited one of the various fine public parks in which two urchins were playing on the high swings. Suddenly one of them fell from quite a height onto the gravel below. His companion immediately slowed down his swing, jumped off and ran to his friend shouting, 'Is ya blodden, Wallie Thompson?' for Wallie was motionless, completely winded. Luckily grown-ups took over to restore him.

The next day Mother left me to return to Dad and all the McLaren family took the train to Bervie, a small salmon fishing hamlet on the East Coast about thirty miles north of Arbroath, a Royal Burgh known for its flax spinning, in Kincardineshire. The McLaren's cottage was very primitive with candles and oil lamps for lighting and a water supply from the adjoining burn.

It was sparsely furnished and I thought lacking in the home comforts to which I was accustomed – I expect I was very homesick. The spartan life was adequate but I was unused to eating porridge with salt and drinking buttermilk, 'So good for children,' I was told, but I found it difficult to adjust.

The sandy beach of Bervie Bay stretched for miles along the coast and a few cottages were clustered near the river, the Bervie Water, which poured down into the sea and there leapt the salmon – a beautiful sight. I enjoyed

Edinburgh Castle

fishing and had accompanied my father many times, but most of the activity in Bervie took place at night when the fishing boats went out and, of course, I was not allowed to go.

Also, one or both of the girls looked after me, often reluctantly, for I think they would have preferred to go out with the young fishermen. The great heat continued for the four weeks we were there and I was very glad when, at the end of the holiday, both Dad and Mum came to take me home.

Before doing so, we spent several days in Edinburgh which I found fascinating with soldiers in Scottish uniforms parading on the castle's historic yard, with John Knox's house, St Giles Cathedral and shops filled with tartan souvenirs and books about the Scottish clans. It was all so interesting to a child and it quite compensated for the boring month at Bervie, though my parents thought I had benefited from the clean sea air and sunshine.

Some twelve years later returning from Norway on the *SY Eileen* we sailed south west past the Orkneys and around Cape Wrath, through the Hebrides visiting Dunoon, Skye, Rhum, Eigg and Muck to Tobermory, a delightful little town, to Mull and Islay. The boys left the ship to shoot seals in Loch Awe, a charming area dotted with ruined castles, but the September weather was atrocious. Fuel was running low, making the yacht very buoyant. I was seasick and glad when we berthed at Gourock at the mouth of the Clyde for the winter overhaul.

In the summer of 1942 John Hoyland, recently drafted with the army, was posted at Helensburgh, about an hour's journey from Glasgow, and his mother Vera suggested that we arrange a holiday on Loch Lomond, the most celebrated and probably the most beautiful lake in Europe; we hoped to have some sailing. The prospect delighted me and we travelled by train, changing several times before arriving on a lovely September evening at the picturesque little hotel on the shore of the loch.

As the hotelier welcomed us, at the end of an exhausting journey, he glanced up at the sky and remarked, 'Maybe a wee drap o' rain coming.' It seemed impossible, but he was right; it poured down continuously for thirteen nights and days. Not having contemplated such weather, we had not taken mackintoshes or galoshes and so it was impossible to move out of doors.

One day I decided to risk it and set off by train to Glasgow where Eric Hall was billeted, arranging to meet him under the station clock in Glasgow Station. On arrival I waited an hour for him to come. Finally, I decided to leave and rushed out of the station to the nearest shop selling rainwear to buy a mackintosh for my return journey to the lake.

It transpired that Eric also waited an hour at another entrance under another clock and that's why we did not meet.

The rain continued and the local inhabitants boasted with glee that their lake had risen nine inches, evidently a record.

As our fortnight's holiday drew to a close, I was determined that we should at least have one steamer trip on the loch; so in spite of the weather we took tickets for the 2.30 boat and at 2.35pm the sun struggled through and we enjoyed a sail at last.

Some years later Bea and I set off by car for a short holiday in the Scottish Lowlands, making our headquarters at a lovely hotel in the Royal Burgh of North Berwick, that fashionable holiday resort where we hoped to have a game of golf on one of the famous links. It was crisp exhilarating weather in early autumn and we toured the Lowland country with great pleasure.

We had entered Scotland at the ancient border town of Berwick-on-Tweed to visit Melrose Abbey not far from Sir Walter Scott's country home at Abbotsford where several of the Waverley Novels were written. Also of course, we saw the famous university campus founded in 1412, the oldest in Scotland, at the Royal Burgh of St Andrews, the headquarters of the Royal and Ancient game of golf.

There is much of historical interest in this town closely connected with John Knox.

☆   ☆   ☆

In 1948 it was my good fortune to go to the Edinburgh International Festival of Music and Drama, perhaps the most prestigious event of its kind in the world. With Bea and another friend I travelled north in her lovely car and spent several busy days at the North British Hotel in Edinburgh, attending various orchestral and chamber music concerts and a memorable production of the *Taming of the Shrew*. There was a spectacular military performance of the *Tattoo* held at night in the castle grounds high above the lovely gardens of Princes Street. We later drove through the Old Town and along the Royal Mile, the beautiful street which links the castle with Holyrood Palace, the Queen's official residence in Scotland.

The Royal Burgh of Edinburgh, the capital city of

31

Scotland, owes much to its superb national setting, overlooked by the dominating mass of Arthur's Seat, a mountain in miniature. The city itself, often described as a modern Athens, is a great educational centre with its famous university and a number of well-known schools, but the world-wide fame of Edinburgh is as a showplace.

The late 18th Century New Town contains broad and stately streets and squares, notably George Street and Charlotte Square with some characteristic Georgian buildings by Robert Adam. Many famous names are associated with the city: Sir Walter Scott and Robert Louis Stevenson were born here and Thackeray, Dickens and Gladstone lectured in the Assembly Rooms.

Apart from St Giles Cathedral erected in the 14th and 15th Centuries and surmounted by the famous Crown steeple, there are many churches of historical interest. A few miles to the west of the city is the spectacular Forth Bridge, built between 1883 and 1890, one of the engineering wonders of the world, which carries the main railway between Edinburgh and Aberdeen, across the Firth of Forth.

Edinburgh is one of the loveliest cities in Europe and its Scottish national war memorial, a shrine and gallery of honour adjoining the castle, a tribute to the fallen of two world wars is quite unique.

No holiday would be complete without a visit to the National Gallery of Paintings which houses a very important and valuable collection of all schools.

It was a wonderful few days packed with interest and activity and we reminisced happily whilst retracing our drive homeward.

In the summer of 1957 I travelled north with Miss Turnbull, my headmistress at Dore and Totley, to spend a few days in her parents' home in Morningside where the family gave me a truly Scottish welcome. We re-visited many familiar haunts in Edinburgh and the Lowlands and I was most interested to observe the changes in the fifty years since my first visit.

Some years later in September I was a guest in Miss Turnbull's own home. Then, amongst many other pursuits, we heard at the Festival a remarkable concert by Yehudi Menuhin and pupils from his violin schools, demonstrating the wonderfully high standard of their tuition and achievements.

What a remarkable capital city!

LANCASHIRE

Liverpool is Lancashire's chief port and its basins and docks cover a water area of six hundred acres, with nearly forty miles of quays.

It is also noted for its magnificent buildings such as the Liver and Cunard Buildings along the seafront which seem to extend a welcome to the great ships arriving from overseas.

Two of the outstanding features of this city are its cathedrals. Both are very impressive, the ancient building from antiquity and the marvellous modern structure for the Roman Catholics which has taken so long to build: it also possesses a famous university and the Blue Coat Chambers dating from 1714.

I once attended a conference of the Incorporated Society of Musicians, of which I was a member, in the premises of Rushworth and Dreaper organ builders, owners of practice studies and a delightful small concert hall suitable for recitals and chamber music.

St George's Hall, the 18th Century town hall and the Walker Art Gallery are also notable, as well as Georgina House in Rodney Street, where Gladstone was born.

My friend Mildred lived for a time on the Wirral Peninsular which separates the mouths of the Rivers Dee and Mersey and during several visits to her home we explored, in my small car, many of the delightful towns and villages in the area including the ancient city of Chester.

Although so many of my schoolfriends lived in Manchester, or in the industrial areas surrounding it, I had few connections with that city or its county.

Manchester, the former Roman station, Mancunium, is now a great cotton and university city, linked to the sea by the Manchester Ship Canal completed in 1894, with fine modern docks.

The cathedral is mainly Perpendicular, having a fine tower and notable woodwork, and there are many interesting churches.

The city was much damaged by bombs, but the Free Trade Hall has been rebuilt; the 15th Century Cheetham's Hospital with its famous history is now a school.

Thomas de Quincey was born in Manchester in 1785.

When I left school, I spent five days attending Owen's College to sit for London Matriculation and did at least see some of the city's cultural aspects – especially the City Art Gallery and Museum, the Henry Watson Music Library and an astounding collection of seventy thousand volumes and three hundred pieces of sheet music at the John Ryland's Library.

But I had weightier matters on my mind, chiefly mathematics papers, never a good subject, and as our hotel was situated at a tram terminus, each night's sleep was disturbed by the constant clang of these great machines being manipulated into position as they returned on their routes.

ISLE OF MAN

After the ordeal at Owen's College, my foster father took me to the Isle of Man for a few day's holiday. We crossed by steamer from Heysham to Douglas on a somewhat blustery day and I was glad to reach our hotel in Ramsey, after an enjoyable electric car ride across the island through Laxey.

The very beautiful Isle of Man lies in the Irish Sea midway between England and Northern Ireland and is only thirty-three miles long and twelve miles broad.

The island, known to the Romans as Mona, possesses much lovely scenery. Its capital, Douglas – a popular holiday resort, contains a great deal of historical interest and several noteworthy churches; old fashioned horse-drawn trams are still a feature.

Laxey Glen is picturesque and from the village begins the mountain railway to Snaefell; where a big wheel was constructed to keep the lead mines free from water.

The giant Quoiting Stone lies on the road between Port St Mary, Port Erin and Castleton, pretty seaside resorts, in the south of the island. I often stayed there when I was a child, but in later years, we preferred Ramsey where we found a pleasant hotel on the seafront.

The island is unique for its system of government; for over a thousand years its decrees have been addressed to the inhabitants at the Tynwald, at an open-air ceremony

36

held every July 5th. It is very interesting to watch this revival, the continuation of ancient customs.

Most people know of the famous Grand Prix motorcycle races which take place annually around the narrow island lanes, but though very exciting to watch, it is terrifying to see the hazards the riders undertake as they negotiate the sharp corners at high speed.

We had planned a relaxing holiday playing golf at Ramsey, but one morning, as we sat under a shady tree on the edge of the fairway to enjoy our sandwiches, my father told me that I was not his daughter; he and his wife had adopted me in 1903 and had brought me up as their own child.

This news was a terrible shock to me, for, although I had little in common with my parents, either in appearance or temperament, I had never imagined the reason for the many differences.

To my questions as to my own family and relatives he had no answer, except that I was born in London.

So, I did not belong to anyone; my whole world disintegrated and all day I was quite benumbed.

When night came and I was alone, the full realization of this news struck me and I could not sleep, troubled by the many problems it raised. But slowly the hours of darkness passed and when the pale finger of dawn touched the sky with opalescent colour, I dressed, crept downstairs, unbolted the doors and stepped into another glorious June morning.

I set off walking along the shore as close to the sea as possible, heedless that the gentle waves of the incoming tide rippled about my feet.

At least, I accepted that, unlike other girls, I had no roots, no background, no security and was probably illegitimate. Henceforth I must rely on my own efforts, for I could expect little or no support from others. In future I must work unceasingly to establish my own independence for I had no family pattern of behaviour.

Some time later that day, I retraced my steps.

Father, anxious that I might still be overwrought, was looking for me on the dunes; I took his hand and together we walked back into the real world.

WELSH BORDER COUNTIES
AND WALES

The counties bordering England and Wales have a special character created by a mixture of the two races with different ideals and culture: Cheshire, Shropshire and Herefordshire are predominantly English, whilst Monmouthshire, the administrative centre, is entirely Welsh.

Cheshire is both agricultural and industrial and its county town, Chester, is one of the most picturesque in Britain, enclosed by the ancient city walls which stand upon Roman and Norman foundations.

These bastions of the former Roman town of Deva are wonderfully preserved, studded with towers and interspersed with ancient gates. The beautiful, mainly 14th Century cathedral of red sandstone, once a Benedictine Abbey, is notable for extensive monastic remains and richly carved woodwork.

The former High Cross destroyed in 1643 was restored and set up in 1946 and there are many lovely old half-timbered houses, interesting churches and hospitals. The Castle is 19th Century with a museum and is now used by the army.

An unique feature of this town is the Rows, a series of galleried arcades outside the first floors of old timbered houses, now used as shops, two of which, Bishop Lloyd's House and God's Provident House, date back to the early 17th Century.

This whole area is full of half-timbered houses and ancient churches, notably in Oswestry, Nantwich and Shrewsbury. The past history of the latter is belied by the academic atmosphere created by one of England's oldest and best known public schools.

Lewis Carroll (the Rev Dodgson), was born at Daresbury.

Church Stretton is an attractive health resort, an area of outstanding beauty, and I clearly remember being awakened in the early morning by the bleating of sheep being driven through the narrow streets of Leominster to market. The Roman Ludlow Castle, now in ruins, is the place from which the two little princes, Edward and his brother, were taken to the Tower of London to suffer death in 1483.

Herefordshire and Monmouthshire contain the beautiful Wye Valley, extending from Hereford to Chepstow at the mouth of the Wye. Its fascinating scenery, undulating fields, orchards and pink-brick timbered farmhouses contrast with the Forest of Dean, where the Romans first dug for iron. Hereford itself contains many historical features, including a chair used by King Stephen, and the Mappa Mundi of 1314, one of the earliest maps in existence.

A tour by car of this lovely area includes Ross-on-Wye, a pretty country town overlooking the river, and Symond's Yat, a famous beauty spot in a narrow loop of the winding Wye in a richly wooded setting which gives a superb view of the river flowing down towards Tintern Abbey.

Chepstow at the mouth of the Wye is dominated by a massive castle perched on a cliff at the junction of the

Wye with the Severn. Although the south coast of Wales is largely industrialized, it possesses wide stretches of countryside still wild and open in spite of its important towns. Newport handles Welsh exports and Cardiff is a great seaport and administrative centre, the chief city in Wales. Its university, Norman castle and civic centre are notable.

Near Swansea, the third great city in industrial South Wales and an important oil port on the Gower Peninsular, is a wild, wooded stretch of very beautiful country where Eileen and I decided to take our yellow labrador for a holiday. We chose to stay at the delightful hotel at the foot of a steep cliff, only accessible down a narrow winding road and, as we had a large car, a Rolls Royce Silver Cloud, negotiation was difficult for there was only a very small parking area at the bottom.

It took some time to overcome these difficulties but at last we were happily settled for the weekend and, despite the problems of ascending the steep road with little space for manoeuvre, we managed to explore the surrounding countryside quite thoroughly.

The unique village of Portmeirion was built by the well known architect Clough Williams Ellis in the Italianate style with houses, churches and a few public buildings each constructed in a separate form. To the architect and builder the creation of this community was the realization of a lifelong dream, and it gave us great pleasure to browse around the pillars and courtyards so reminiscent of the classical era.

Driving westward we reached Kidwelly and Carmarthen, each with its ruined castle, and by the coast is the charming resort of Tenby, a useful centre for excursions to Pembroke Castle, Milford Haven and St Davids, the smallest cathedral city (12th Century) in the kingdom; the ruins of the 13th Century Bishop's Palace are

The Amis Reunis, Portmeirion, Wales

extensive.

Central Wales provides mountain scenery on a grand scale intersected by green and fertile valleys among which roads wind in a sinuous sometimes exciting way and these mountains sweep down to the sea creating a background to a lovely coastline.

Aberystwyth, situated on Cardigan Bay, is a pleasure resort as well as a university town. It is not far from the picturesque upper reaches of the River Wye and Builth Wells.

Llandrindod Wells, one of the best spas in Great Britain, is noted for its chalybeate springs and continuing northwards we come to Aberdovey where the Outward Bound School provides adventure training for boys.

The picturesque heights of Cader Idris lie to the south and to the east is Dolgelly where the curfew is still rung nightly; to the north lies the magnificent 13th Century Castle of Harlech.

The north coast of Wales is best known for the popular seaside resorts such as Conway, and Caernarvon with two imposing castles, one at either end of the Menai Straits, Llandudno, Colwyn Bay, Rhyl and Prestatyn.

I spent one summer holiday helping in a café in Colwyn Bay and have many happy memories of excursions in the well known holiday areas.

I worked for my board and lodging, plus any tips I received, but they were few and far between and I was grateful for the odd sixpence when it was offered.

Sunday was our free day and on a scorching summer's afternoon, Vera and I, returning with the children from a picnic in the Austin 7, saw a strange sight; a group of people standing in the roadway by an abandoned car.

There were two smartly dressed men and a short stout figure, almost square in build, arrayed in a gorgeous gown, the bodice of which was embroidered in sequins.

There she stood stretching out her fat little be-ringed fingers to stop a passing car, for traffic in those days was sparse and infrequent.

It was the famous queen of opera, Madame Tetrazzini, who had been billed to sing in Llandudno that evening and, as I slowed down, the diamonds on her hands and neck flashed in the summer sunshine.

As I stopped, a few feet from the handsome limousine broken down by the kerb, I was immediately surrounded by her entourage, her Italian manager, a small dark man, and a younger one, probably her accompanist, who rushed up gesticulating and excited.

Would we escort Madame into town? Time was running out and she would be late for her concert; they begged us to help.

But Madame intervened. 'But this auto is too small. I could not fit into it.'

True the Austin 7 of that era was only scheduled to carry a load of twenty-eight stones and we already had our full complement.

What was to be done? I finally suggested that we continue on our way and call at the first available police station for help.

So we left them with expressions of, 'Grazia Signorina, we will await the polizei,' and we called at a sleepy police office not far along the road to report the incident.

Next morning we read in the local newspaper that she had fulfilled her engagement triumphantly, in spite of delay of a punctured tyre.

☆ ☆ ☆

Later that year, I attended a summer music school organized by the Incorporated Society of Musicians and held at Howell's School, Denbigh, set in lovely scenery.

The accommodation was good but the music programme left much to be desired.

Many of the students taking part in the courses were already pupils of professors and teachers lecturing and demonstrating, consequently there were few opportunities for the unknown student not associated with the élite. Most of the places for master seminars and individual tuition appeared to have been allotted before we arrived in Denbigh, so that the outsider just tagged along behind.

Fortunately, I had my Austin 7 and could spend much of the two week session in exploring the area of the Clewyd Valley.

☆ ☆ ☆

In the early 1920s I discovered a charming little country pub situated near Holywell where the shrine of St Winefride is one of the traditional wonders of Wales. The tiny cathedral of St Asaph, the smallest in England and Wales, founded in the 6th Century, was destroyed by Owen Glendower in 1402, largely rebuilt in the 15th Century, and has an 18th Century choir. The delightful little inn was on a wayside track tucked away from the main road, and there Hilda and I spent many short holidays.

The front entrance led to a small bar with seasoned oak beams and benches forming an inglenook beside a blazing fire which lit up the shining brass hunting trophies and other decorations on the walls. The warm gentle lighting from oil lamps created a cosy atmosphere, a hospitable and welcoming retreat from the cold and wet; a real haven of peace.

ISLAND OF ANGLESEY

The lovely Isle of Anglesey is separated from North West Wales by a narrow channel bridge at Bangor by Telford's great suspension bridge carrying road traffic. Not far away stands Stephenson's Britannia Railway Bridge serving the railway system. Nearby is a statue of Nelson and a monument to the Marquis of Anglesey who was second in command at the battle of Waterloo.

There are many charming holiday resorts on the island; Beaumaris, with its fine 13th Century moated castle and interesting 13th to 15th Century church, and Rhosneiger and Trearrdur Bay on Holy Island on the north west coast. Holyhead, the port with a regular steamer service to Ireland, contains a church founded in the 7th Century with a wall thought to be Roman. On the mountain are traces of ancient fortifications.

PART

2

DERBYSHIRE AND
THE PEAK DISTRICT

I lived in Derbyshire for about forty-five years, from the age of ten, for the southern boundaries of Sheffield reached into the county.

In the early days our only contact with the town was by train and the few resident businessmen and shoppers commuted when necessary walking to and from the village station, unless Jimmy's one-horse bus was available. This vehicle plied between the local station and the Cross Scythes Inn, if and when there were enough customers to fill it; if not, you sat in the open waggonette, often in the rain, until the next train brought some more passengers. It was often quicker to walk.

Although my school was near the station, my parents discouraged the use of Jimmy's horse bus, on the grounds that his language was too colourful, unsuitable for the ears of a young child.

There were few motor vehicles and only the wealthy could afford a car, but my friend's parents owned a Hupmobile which sometimes took us farther afield, as a great treat.

There are many beauty spots on the fringe of the Peak District within easy distance of Sheffield, such as Chatsworth House, the famous palatial 17th Century

Chesterfield Church

50

home of the Dukes of Devonshire with the beauty of its grounds and water gardens, its superb collection of pictures and its historical links with the unhappy Mary, Queen of Scots, who was detained there.

Not far away is Haddon Hall, 12th to 15th Century, a fortified mediaeval house of great beauty and the property of the Dukes of Rutland. From there Dorothy Vernon made her romantic elopement with John Manners in the 16th Century.

In the autumn of 1939, Vera leased a smallholding in the Barlow valley to provide experience for her son, who wished to become a farmer.

Situated at the foot of a narrow winding road the stone-built farmhouse, perhaps a hundred years old, stood on a level patch of green surrounded by cattle, pigs and chickens creating a picturesque setting.

But, after Christmas the winter became severe. It was increasingly difficult for the two of them to heat the isolated farmhouse, and tend the animals in snow and ice; extra help seemed impossible to obtain and Vera became even more frail. In the following September, the outbreak of war and John's call-up into the army seemed a legitimate excuse for ending an unsuccessful venture.

The picturesque market town of Bakewell nearby, is famous, not only for its luscious tarts not found elsewhere, but for its interesting 12th to 14th Century church, and other 16th Century buildings.

In 1940, I bought a small school in Bakewell, well situated at the rear of a doctor's house on the road to Haddon Hall.

There were about twenty junior pupils, accommodated very comfortably in the doctor's re-furbished outhouses and well managed by a couple of experienced teachers and I became most interested in developing it. This excellent wartime activity provided a weekly

Bakewell well dressing

diversion allowing me to check the children's progress and enjoy an excellent lunch with them behind the greengrocer's shop.

This little school had a distinct personality of its own. It was useless to attempt any changes, even improvements, as the children were from the countryside, of prosperous farmers, professional and county men, who resented any form of change. They would grow up in stereotyped country fashion and who could blame them?

Many of the villages are famous for the annual well dressing displays which encourage competition at Whitsuntide amongst the small communities.

The village well, often intact with its pumping system, is decorated with a religious picture created in flowers. Many thousands of petals are used to weave the scenery and the figures, creating a magnificent tapestry. The villagers compete in skill and artistry with remarkable success. Perhaps the most famous display is that at Tissington near Buxton, but Hope, Castleton, Monyash, Youlgreave and many others pass down these hereditary features from generation to generation.

The little village of Eyam, in the Peak District, is famous for its fight against the Great Plague of 1665, which was conveyed to it from London in a parcel of clothing.

The villagers isolated themselves to avoid the spread of infection to neighbouring areas, and were cared for devotedly by their vicar, the Rev Mompesson. In the churchyard stands an ancient Runic Cross; there is also a Georgian rectory and a fine manor house of 1676.

The Peak District is an area of moorland hills intersected by steep rock-strewn dales, through which streams of great beauty wind their picturesque way. In Dovedale, one of these valleys, Isaac Walton (1593-1683) fished with his friend Cotton, joint-author of the *Compleat Angler,* the classic treatise on the art of angling.

The whole of the Peak District is served with good roads, making its beauties easily accessible from surrounding cities and towns.

Peveril Castle in the Winnats near Castleton is an ancient ruined fortress immortalized by Sir Walter Scott in his novel *Peveril of the Peak,* and nearby are the famous Blue John Mines which attract many thousands of tourists each year.

Buxton, one of the best-known spas in England, a thousand feet above sea level, was made famous by the Romans for the healing properties of its natural water, the thermal and chalybeate springs, and is a centre for the treatment of rheumatism. It is an attractive town, with pleasing Georgian 18th Century architecture, built to enhance the cult of the natural springs.

Between 1915 and 1920 I spent the years at The Grange boarding school in Buxton, an academy convenient for the wartime safety of many girls who would otherwise have been educated abroad.

There, I learned to appreciate Buxton's many amenities such as the winter sports and the beauty of the town and its surrounding districts.

If our behaviour warranted it, we were allowed to attend concerts in the municipal gardens three times a week during the summer term, parading from school to the pavilion in our black silk coats, white gloves and school hats. These excursions did much to foster our musical training for at such excellent concerts we heard most of the national and international musical celebrities of the time who would not otherwise have been available in the provinces.

After Neville Chamberlain's meeting with Adolf Hitler at Munich in 1938, many Britons were reassured that war with Germany was not imminent but in 1939 there was little doubt that it would come and cautious people began to make preparations for possible evacuation from the cities.

My friend Vera Hoyland, bought a lovely little house in Hope about fourteen miles from Sheffield to accommodate her elderly father and her two children, and during the next few years I spent many happy holidays there, at The Green.

Its situation on a sloping hillside, overlooking the charming village, was really delightful, surrounded by meadows against a backcloth of wooded hills and the peaceful idyllic environment was rarely disturbed by sirens warning of enemy air raids.

However, one Sunday evening in early December 1940, about 7.15 pm, I was enjoying a snack before leaving for home when the distant wail of the siren seemed audible. I put on my outdoor clothes and whilst standing outside on the step, distinctly heard the warning from several directions. Having said a hasty farewell I left, for I was anxious to reach home if possible before the raid began. Taking the narrow lane by the church to meet the main road, I was stopped by the flashing lamp of the village policeman who enquired where I was going and why, to which I replied that I had children in my care and must travel to Totley for I had never left them in an emergency.

'My orders are to allow no-one to drive except with permission; you must turn off your lights and drive in the dark and be most careful for you will meet heavy and dangerous traffic on the road,' and with this cheering message he set me on my way.

As I joined the main road from Manchester I groped along by the kerb for we were not allowed to use headlamps and heavy lorries carrying anti-aircraft guns, ammunition, soldiers, hospital equipment and other necessities flashed past me, also without lights, and on two occasions found their way into the ditch.

It was a nightmare drive and although I knew the road well I was very thankful to arrive home, some time later, without a puncture or a collision, for there were many during the night. However, I found the staff and children safe, together with a group of neighbours in our air raid shelters drinking cocoa and listening to the gramophone as they prepared for bed in the shelters.

On the previous Thursday night Sheffield had been subjected to a severe raid which destroyed a large section of the city so severely that two days later, the King and Queen visited the disaster area. The terrific noise and gunfire lighting up the sky seemed to usher in another dreadful night and we prepared for a long session, but at midnight there was sudden silence. The raiders had been recalled. The moon came up and I walked out to check on the possible damage to our property, leaving the children fast asleep in the shelters.

THE MIDLANDS

Derby, the county town, is an important commercial centre, well known for its engineering and manufacturing, much of it for the railway system.

The county hall has a façade dating from 1660. There are some fine Georgian houses and the Assembly Rooms date from 1763-4.

The cathedral rebuilt in 1725, has a fine 16th Century tower, a screen of 18th Century ironwork and some interesting tombs.

There is a restored bridge chapel on the 18th Century river bridge and the Royal Crown Derby porcelain factory can be visited.

Derby's strategic situation in the centre of England has played an important part in our history throughout the ages as a focal rallying point.

Chesterfield, an interesting market town and a centre of the coal and iron industry, is noted for the twisted lead-covered spire surmounted on the 14th Century All Saint's Parish Church; this leans nearly eight feet out of true at the summit and is clearly seen from the railway line to Sheffield. George Stephenson lived here and was buried in Trinity Church.

☆ ☆ ☆

To the east lies Nottingham, notable for its production of lace and hosiery; its 17th Century castle standing on a rock overlooking the town is now a museum famous for an underground passage known as Mortimer's Hole, by which Edward III entered in 1330 to arrest his mother and Earl Mortimer, who murdered his father.

In Castle Gate there are some Georgian houses and several churches and inns of note, including the Palatial City Hall and 18th Century Willoughby House.

☆ ☆ ☆

Southwell is a quiet little town distinguished by a beautiful Norman Minster, completed in 1150 – a very fine example of Norman Perpendicular work, and ruins of an Archbishop's Palace are still extant together with many interesting buildings. In this town Charles I surrendered to the Scots in 1646.

William Booth, founder of the Salvation Army, was born here.

☆ ☆ ☆

Nearby is Newark-on-Trent, a pleasant market town with a fine Perpendicular church, containing some notable brasses; it also boasts the ruins of a large castle of the 12th to 15th Century and some fine Georgian houses, a wide market square and old inns.

Not far away lie the Dukeries, the spacious parks of Welbeck, Clumber, Worksop and Thoresby, which belonged to the Dukes of Portland, Newcastle, Norfolk and Kingston.

Especially notable are the extensive underground

galleries and reception rooms constructed by the Duke of Portland in the 19th Century.

EAST MIDLANDS
AND LINCOLNSHIRE

I know little of Lincolnshire, except for visits to the village of Fillingham, chiefly notable for Samson's Castle dated 1770, which is still inhabited and in good repair: John Wycliffe was rector at the village church from 1361 to 1365.

The first time I drove from Grantham to Fillingham I was quite astounded by the rapid change of scenery, for I found myself travelling across low-lying marshland intersected by numerous 'drains' which obviously filtered the bog for agricultural purposes.

As these narrow waterways were adjacent to roads and footpaths, I could envisage great hazard to travellers on these routes in darkness or poor visibility.

The county town, Lincoln, in the centre of the area possesses a magnificent 11th to 15th Century cathedral, reputedly destroyed by an earthquake in 1185 and rebuilt by Bishop Hugh of Avalon. The cathedral library built by Wren in 1674 contains a copy of **Magna Carta**, and many examples of wood-carving and windows with an important collection of diocesan plate.

The Norman castle was founded by William the Conqueror and there are many buildings of great antiquity and interest, including the old High Bridge which carries a row of timbered houses.

Near the coast is Boston a charming ancient sea port of particular interest to Americans, for here the leaders of the Pilgrim Fathers were tried in 1607 for attempting to leave the country. The tower, more than two hundred and seventy feet high, of St Botolph's parish church, known as Boston Stump, can be seen for miles across this flat countryside. Midway between Boston and Lincoln is the charming little spa of Woodhall, with its pump room and bathing establishment, situated among pines and rich in bromo-iodine springs.

There are a number of seaside resorts including bracing Skegness, Mablethorpe, Cleethorpes and Grimsby, the largest fishing port in the world, all of which are notable for long stretches of golden sand and safe bathing facilities.

THE MIDLANDS, LEICESTERSHIRE AND RUTLAND

The county of Leicestershire is well known for some of the best foxhunting centred around Melton-Mowbray and for its meat pies and stilton cheese. Famous packs of hounds such as Belvoir, Cottesmore, Pytchley and Fernie are based here and the terrain over which they hunt is undulating grassland intersected by stiff fences and yawning brooks.

In this area is Leicester, the largest city with a prominent university and many industries related to hosiery and footwear.

Once a Roman walled station there is much of interest in the relics of Roman work, beside the church of St Nicholas, a Roman pavement under the central railway station and Roman masonry in the Jewry Wall. There are many relics of the Norman period, and the 14th Century Guildhall together with historic churches are of considerable interest.

My association with the city spans the years from 1907 to 1960, during which I visited friends there at least once a year, and explored the area quite thoroughly. They moved into a lovely house at Alexton, near Oakham, the capital of Rutland, most interesting for its famous public school and the 12th to 15th Century church, and remains of the castle with its splendid Norman banqueting hall. We spent much time with the hunting community in this delightful area.

EAST ANGLIA

The cathedral city of Norwich was once the centre of the worsted trade but now specializes in footwear. Its cathedral is largely Norman with 15th Century choir stalls and cloisters and Edith Cavell's grave at the south east corner of the building. The Bishop's Palace is 12th to 15th Century and The Close contains some charming old houses.

Two dominant features of the city are the cathedral noted for its lovely spire and flying buttresses and the restored castle which now houses a well equipped museum and art gallery displaying examples of the Norwich School of painting.

Norwich possesses many churches: in 1086 AD there were sixty-nine, but many were destroyed by the German air raids of the Second World War. Only thirty-four still remain. Suckling House, 15th Century, and the Guildhall of chequered flints built in 1407, are outstanding old buildings. Nelson was a pupil at the Old Grammar School and Elizabeth Fry, the first great prison reformer, lived in Earlham Hall, now part of the University of East Anglia. The Music House, mainly Elizabethan, retains some Norman work and is now a centre for amateur musicians.

Norfolk is remarkable for its Broads, a series of inland waterways made up of lagoons connected by rivers which extend for many miles through enchanting scenery similar to the Dutch landscape. It is an ideal centre for yachting, free from the hazards of the open sea and attracts many thousands of tourists each year.

In the early 1930s I spent several holidays with Emmie and her friends from Norwich in a bungalow near Potter Heigham, where they kept their boat. Sharing the chores, we slept in the bungalow and sailed throughout the days, visiting other centres such as Wroxham, Great Yarmouth and Norwich the county town – lovely carefree holidays.

The district lying between Norwich, Lowestoft and Sea Palling, contains more than thirty 'broads' of different sizes which, together with rivers and streams, provide two hundred miles of inland waterways, unique in Great Britain.

The Broadland churches are noted for their wonderful mediaeval painted screens.

Some years later I spent more time in Norwich at an Independent Schools Conference and much enjoyed its beautiful mediaeval streets, ancient buildings and waterways.

Great Yarmouth on Breydon Water possesses a seafront of about five miles, beautiful gardens, two piers, some notable churches and remains of town walls and gates. Some interesting houses in the narrow Rows have been restored and are in constant use.

The town is associated with one of the greatest of Charles Dickens' novels *David Copperfield* as the home of the Peggotty family.

Norfolk boasts of many well known seaside resorts, Cromer and Sheringham are perhaps best known and Hilda and I spent a holiday at the latter a number of times to enjoy the golf. Nearby is West Runton where I often stayed with one of my pupils who had retired there;

it is a beautifully wooded area and contains a Roman Camp.

There are many interesting mansions in this district.

Hunstanton, facing The Wash, is more modern, though its Hall dates from the early 16th Century.

King's Lynn, a busy inland port near The Wash, is connected to the sea by the River Ouse; its Tudor Guildhall of black flint and white stone and the 15th Century Greyfriars Tower are two noteworthy buildings in the town and there are many interesting Georgian and earlier houses. Fanny Burney was born here in 1752.

Norfolk contains large and famous country houses and the grounds are open to the public. Sandringham, the 19th Century home of the Royal Family since Edward VII, and the East Holkham Hall belonging to the Earl of Leicester, famous for his agricultural experimentation, are not far from King's Lynn. Near Cromer is Blickling Hall, the beautiful Jacobean mansion, birthplace of Anne Boleyn, bequeathed to the National Trust by the Earl of Lothian.

Along the coast are a number of popular resorts. Lowestoft with its two piers and quaint narrow lanes called Scores, leading from the High Street to the beach; Southwold with the sea on one side, open heath on the other and the lighthouse in the centre of the town, offers all the facilities which tourists could demand. A little farther south is Aldeburgh, now world famous for its annual festival of opera and concerts. Founded by Sir Benjamin Britten and Peter Pears, it is increasingly important, but unfortunately I have never managed to visit it.

Continuing south is Felixstowe on the River Orwell, and down the river is Ipswich, the county town of Suffolk associated with Mr Pickwick's visit to the Great White Horse Hotel. It is historically very interesting, the birthplace of Cardinal Wolsey and home of Gainsborough.

On the coast near Felixstowe lies Harwich, a quaint old sea port, the terminus for passenger services to Antwerp, the Hook of Holland, Hamburg and the Baltic ports, from which I have sailed on a number of occasions. It was known to Nelson who stayed at the Three Cups Hotel.

Frinton-on-Sea is a small exclusive seaside resort with good golf. Walton-on-the-Naze and Clacton almost at the mouth of The Thames are very popular resorts, easily accessible to London.

A short distance inland is Colchester, one of the most ancient and interesting towns in England. Captured by the Romans, it was retrieved in 61 AD by Queen Boadicea and later became the home of 'Old King Cole'. Colchester contains many very important buildings including its Norman castle built of Roman materials, but is now chiefly famous for its production of roses and oysters.

Farther inland lies the charming town of Bury St Edmunds where in 870 AD the Danes martyred the saintly Edmund, last King of Anglia, who had refused to renounce the Christian faith.

The 14th Century Abbey Gateway, the Abbot's Residence and Bridge and the Dove House are all that remain of the great 11th Century monastery and in St Mary's Church, noted for its roof and glass, is the grave of Mary Tudor, daughter of King Henry VIII.

Cambridge, the famous university city situated in the fens, is one of the great architectural glories of England. King's College Chapel built by Henry VI can be described as perfect, and so is the music produced by its choristers. As we had several ex-pupils studying there over the years, we often spent a few days visiting them in their colleges of which there are seventeen; the oldest, Peterhouse, was founded in 1281.

Staying at the University Arms which commands a fine view, we explored the beauties of the town and the lovely scene of the 'Backs', where at the rear of the colleges the gardens slope down to the River Cam. Cambridge is also a good centre for sightseeing.

Ely contains a superb cathedral dating from 1083, dominating the surrounding plain, the King's School, where Edward the Confessor received his education, and the 15th Century Bishop's Palace.

There are associations with Hereward the Wake and Oliver Cromwell and his family lived at the Old Vicarage for ten years.

At Newmarket, the headquarters of English racing since 1603, are trained most of the valuable thorough-breds in the country and here the Two Thousand Guineas and One Thousand Guineas, two of the five classic races are staged. King James I, Charles I and Charles II are associated with the town.

The inland town of Wisbech on the River Nene, known for its fruit, bulbs and market gardening has also many beautiful buildings such as the Octagon House and the Bank House and other fine Georgian houses of the Dutch type.

Farther to the north east is Peterborough with its magnificent Norman cathedral in which Catherine of Aragon lies buried.

Northampton is known mainly for the manufacture of boots and shoes, but it contains the Church of the Holy Sepulchre, one of the four round Norman churches in England; and Eleanor Cross, one of the three remaining original crosses set up by Edward I to mark the halting places of the funeral procession of his wife, Eleanor of Castille, to Westminster Abbey in 1290.

On my way southwards I stayed occasionally in Northampton with a friend, the headmaster of the Grammar School, who lived near the lovely expanse of playing fields.

THE WEST MIDLANDS

Bristol is a famous inland sea port and university city, which requires the navigation of seven miles of the River Avon before a ship reaches the Bristol Channel.

In past centuries Bristol was the centre of England's slave trade with America but much earlier in 1497 John Cabot, and his son Sebastian, sailed from Bristol in the *Matthew* and eventually discovered the mainland of America.

This city contains many fine old buildings, the most beautiful of which is the perpendicular parish church of St Mary Redcliffe, much admired by Queen Elizabeth I.

There is a wealth of historical and architectural interest in this city. The Methodist Chapel, 1739, the largest in the world, was built by John Wesley and above it are the rooms where he and his preachers lived and worked.

Both Southey and Chatterton were born here.

To the north beside the River Severn is the county capital of Gloucester, a former Roman city whose Perpendicular cathedral contains magnificent Norman vaulting and fan tracery as well as the tomb of the unfortunate King Edward II, murdered by his wife Isabella in 1327. Bishop Hooper was martyred here in 1555.

I have stayed many times at the New Inn, an ancient 15th Century galleried pilgrims' hostelry. The Three

Choirs Music Festival takes place every third year in the city, and the famous Gloucester bell foundry, transferred to London in 1828, cast more than four thousand five hundred church bells.

Tewkesbury possesses a magnificent ancient abbey, outside which are still played mediaeval 'Miracle' plays. In 1471 the young Lancastrian Prince of Wales was murdered in the abbey after the savage Battle of Tewkesbury.

There are many picturesque old houses and inns and the watermill still functioning, is featured in *John Halifax Gentleman.*

After the purchase of my Austin 7 in 1926, I decided to invite my Latin tutor, Miss Robertshaw, to join me on a trip to the Cotswolds. We stayed for a night en route at Lichfield, a quiet city known for the birth and work of the famous lexicographer, Dr Samuel Johnson.

The early English cathedral is a massive, elegant building of red sandstone situated by the picturesque river and is the only church in England which has three spires, forming a notable landmark.

Continuing through Warwick, the huge 14th Century castle situated on the banks of the River Avon dominates the town. Built in 915 AD it possesses a fine collection of paintings, armour and furniture and is an important tourist attraction, even when the family is in residence.

The town itself has many half-timbered buildings one of the most beautiful of which is Lord Leycester's Hospital for veteran soldiers, founded in 1383 as a Guildhall.

Walter Savage Landor was born at the County Hall in 1775 and Warwick School founded in 914 was re-founded by Henry VIII in 1545.

Royal Leamington Spa adjoining Warwick, an inland health resort, is a modern attractive spa, noted for the treatment of rheumatism and for the training of guide dogs for the blind. Nathaniel Hawthorne worked here.

We travelled down to Evesham where we made our headquarters for a couple of weeks at a charming hotel, the Mansion House, whose grounds swept down to the river. It is interesting to note that first class accommodation in a spacious bedroom with full board overlooking the landing stage, including a five course dinner, could be obtained for 15/- (75p) per day.

An attractive market town with notable abbey and churches, famous for its fruit and vegetables, it has retained the character of a small village and is an excellent centre for the exploration of the Cotswold towns and villages.

It is the third week in April when the fruit trees in the Vale of Evesham are in full bloom and nothing is more beautiful than to travel through miles of orchards covered in white and pink blossom.

The gently rolling hills and charming villages, built in Tudor times of the local honey-coloured stone, are well named. Moreton-in-the-Marsh with the Fosse Way, famous for its main street; Stow-on-the-Wold, a hill-top town; Bourton-on-the-Water on the River Windrush which is crossed by miniature stone bridges; Shipton-under-Wychwood. There are many others of great beauty, especially Broadway where at the Lygon Arms, a favourite hostelry, I have spent many happy holidays.

Burford is a very picturesque Cotswold town consisting largely of one tree-lined street with old houses and inns. The fine Norman to Perpendicular church was notable in the Civil War when in 1649 Cromwell trapped a number of mutineers inside it.

On various occasions I have stayed in each of the chief hotels – the mediaeval Lamb and the 16th Century Bay

Tree, each of equal merit. There is much of interest in this delightful town.

Fish Hill, more than a thousand feet high, rises above the village of Broadway, famous for its picturesque old houses.

At Bibury are the picturesque Cotswold stone cottages known as Arlington Row.

We had stopped for a picnic lunch in a leafy lane near Bibury when another vintage Rolls Royce drew up about fifty yards from ours and from it tumbled five children aged from five to twelve years. As is customary with owners of old cars, who chat about technical details of common interest, we greeted the parents, who told us that their car, a 1925 Rolls Royce, was the most economical model they could buy to transport the family in comfort with plenty of room. Quite a testimony to the 'red emblem'.

Chipping Campden, Chipping Norton and Chipping Sodbury are three beautiful little Cotswold towns of mediaeval beauty.

The market town of Cirencester, capital of the Cotswolds and once the Roman town of Corinium, is notable for its fine market place and beautiful perpendicular church, built in the 16th Century by the local guilds. Stroud, engaged in the cloth trade and manufacture of pianos is not far from Painswick with its ninety-nine yew trees, a beautiful characteristic little town in a hillside setting.

The waters of Cheltenham Spa, discovered in the 18th Century, have made it famous for the treatment of rheumatism. It is also an educational centre, and well known for the Festival of Contemporary British Music and the Arts. The Georgian architecture and some fine Regency houses bear witness to the town's popularity amongst people of that era. Gustav Holst was born here in 1874.

Stratford-on-Avon is an attractive country town usually packed with tourists of all nationalities anxious to pay tribute to the greatest of playwrights, born here in 1564.

During the next thirteen years until the outbreak of World War II, I spent my April holiday in the Cotswolds with various friends and from 1945 I escorted a party of sixth-formers each year for a few days break to attend Shakespeare's birthday celebrations at Stratford-on-Avon. We travelled either by train or hired a small bus and enjoyed as many performances of his plays as were produced within our five day's visit.

We all stayed in a delightful Elizabethan house in Chapel Street, opposite the Grammar School of 1483, where Shakespeare was educated. Our landlady, Mrs Johnson, accustomed to school parties, provided excellent accommodation with breakfast and an evening meal which enabled us to spend the days in sightseeing both in Stratford and in the surrounding countryside.

On the Birthday Sunday we always attended the service at the parish church of the Holy Trinity on the banks of the River Avon, when leading actors at the theatre read the lessons and everyone took a floral offering to Shakespeare's tomb.

Nearby is the Shakespeare Memorial Theatre where the annual festival of plays takes place. The exterior of the building was much criticized when it was first erected, but it has certainly mellowed with the years and merits affection and respect.

The old ivy-covered theatre close at hand, destroyed by fire in 1926 and now rebuilt, offers a programme of Elizabethan plays contemporary with Shakespeare.

For the birthday celebrations the whole area is en fête with flags and bunting everywhere and a famous representative of every nation stands by to unfurl his country's flag before joining the procession of notabilities; we saw famous heads of state and celebrities in this way.

The ancient Knot Garden at New Place was lovely with flowers and we always spent some time at Anne Hathaway's cottage in Shottery.

Throughout the years I have had many associations with Stratford-on-Avon. As a teenager I had the honour of meeting the famous novelist Marie Corelli at a reception in her home, Mason Croft, which was eventually bought by Americans, demolished and finally rebuilt in the USA. She was an interesting and colourful personality.

More recently I have visited regularly my friend Muffie, an historian living in Shottery in a beautiful Elizabethan cottage almost opposite that of Anne Hathaway. In her own lovely garden which Muffie still tends we can escape from the hurly-burly of modern life.

Amongst places of interest near Stratford are Compton Wynyates, a lovely historic Tudor mansion belonging to the Marquess of Northampton; Charlecote Park, an Elizabethan house in the grounds of which young Shakespeare is reputed to have poached deer, and Stanton and Stanway where in April the spring flowers are at their best.

En route to Stratford we always had a break at Kenilworth to see the remains of the vast castle where Queen Elizabeth's favourite, the Earl of Leicester, entertained her so lavishly.

Worcester cathedral, early English to Perpendicular, built on the River Severn upon the foundations of many earlier churches, is host in rotation with the cathedrals of Hereford and Gloucester to the world-famous Three

Choirs Festival. The city itself contains many fine old houses and buildings dating from mediaeval times. The Royal Porcelain works contain a museum of Worcester China.

Not far from Worcester lies Droitwich Spa where radioactive springs have provided their curative properties since Roman times, and where we often stayed to alleviate my foster father's arthritis.

Broadheath, the birthplace of Sir Edward Elgar, still contains memorabilia of England's most famous composer.

Edward Winslow who sailed in the *Mayflower* and eventually became Governor of Massachusetts was baptized in St Peter's Church.

The festival in Malvern Priory Church, noted for its 15th Century glass, depicts the Vision of Piers Plowman, the 14th Century poet.

There are several Malverns situated on the slopes of the Malvern Hills, but Great Malvern is not only a noted health resort, but has become famous in recent years for another Festival of Drama dedicated to Bernard Shaw, many of whose plays were first produced there. It was also beloved by Sir Edward Elgar, who made his home nearby.

Ledbury is an attractive old market town, the birthplace of John Masefield.

In North Warwickshire is situated England's second city, Birmingham, one of the most important industrial centres in the country, reputed to contain one thousand five hundred different industries within the city's boundaries, but specializing in metal work, jewellery and motor vehicles.

It is said that it can supply any article which may be required.

In addition the city possesses an art gallery which

76

houses one of the most important exhibits outside London and its library contains the largest collection of work on Shakespeare ever assembled, numbering approximately twenty-five thousand items.

Its university is famous and the cathedral of 1711 has chancel windows by Burne-Jones. The ancient Bull Ring in the city centre has been well developed.

After the close of World War II my cousin Hilda and I decided to take a holiday in Cornwall in my Austin 7 but before we could do so we had to assemble as many cans of petrol as we could obtain for an overall journey of more than a thousand miles. At that time petrol was severely rationed but, by saving our coupons and with help from friends we managed to gather a full tank, plus thirteen gallons in tins, which we packed into the very limited space with our luggage and food for the journey,

We left home about 6 o'clock one spring evening and arrived in Birmingham about 8.30 in pouring rain. We found near our hotel a car park which was merely a bombed site and I stayed with the car and its precious load, whilst Hilda checked into the hotel. After a while she returned and I drove to the main entrance of the hotel, unloaded the luggage and began to carry in the thirteen one gallon tins. The reception area was only dimly lit and hotel staff at that time in very short supply, so we easily packed everything into the lift which took us to our bedroom where we stowed the cans in the wardrobe.

I returned to re-park the empty car whilst Hilda organized the supper we had brought with us; we made some coffee and went to bed, exhausted.

Some hours later we were suddenly awakened by the opening of the bedroom door. The light was switched on and there stood a man, only half-clothed in his underwear. I sat upright at once. 'What is the meaning of this?' I said sternly and he muttered something about the wrong room and went away. Perhaps the night porter was looking for a nap in what he thought was an empty room.

The sudden opening of the bedroom door shook the wardrobe and the petrol cans were displaced, so these incidents disturbed sleep for the remainder of the night.

After breakfast next morning we brought down the petrol cans and I fetched the car, leaving Hilda to pay the bill, prior to re-packing all the luggage. As she brought down the last can, the hall porter appeared looking troubled, 'You can't bring petrol into this hotel, it's not safe,' he protested, eyeing the cans askance.

'Well, they've been here all night, but they're going out now,' she retorted as I entered the hotel lobby. He did not dare to help us.

☆ ☆ ☆

East of Birmingham lies Coventry, an historic city and centre of the automobile and cycle industries, as well as an important producer of artificial silk. Historically, it is known for the ride of naked Lady Godiva through the streets in an attempt to placate her husband, Earl Leofric.

Coventry suffered much in the air raids of World War II in 1940, when the beautiful cathedral was totally destroyed except for the altar and its crucifix, which have been retained as a memorial. Two days later the city was visited by King George VI and his Queen which brought great comfort to the townspeople. I happened to be in the city on the following day, just before Christmas, and witnessed the anguished reaction of the populace,

78

grieving at such terrible devastation.

After the war the cathedral was rebuilt, retaining part of the bombed site of the ancient building as historical testimony, but some of the modern paintings and sculpture have elicited much criticism.

The University of Warwick has been established here and Dame Ellen Terry was born in Coventry,

From the eastern slopes of the Cotswolds the River Thames flows on its way to Oxford, ancient and picturesque, one of the most beautiful of English cities.

The colleges, some of which are five hundred years old, are the glory of Oxford. Magdalen is among the most beautiful, its graceful tower guarding the eastern entrance to the city, and Christ Church College whose chapel is Oxford's cathedral.

Each college has its garden including a sacred grass lawn on which only the famous may tread and the architecture of the buildings is quite unique in its beauty. there are churches and inns of great antiquity and a number of fine houses.

About 9 am one September morning Bea and I stood on the wharf at Folly Bridge waiting to board a Salter's steamship for a six-day cruise on the River Thames.

The early mist rising from the river was gradually being dissipated by the sun which promised a fine day. In a few minutes we boarded this attractive boat with our luggage and settled down on deck for the sail. Slowly we glided to the first lock, to Iffley, Abingdon Bridge, to Goring, Mapledurham and Reading where we arrived at 6.15 pm to find good accommodation and an excellent dinner awaiting us.

On the following morning we left Caversham about 10 am, sailing to Henley, Marlow, Cookham, Boulter's Bridge and Bray in lovely weather, arriving in Windsor at

6.15.

Next day, we left via Staines, Chertsey, Shepperton and Molesly, arriving in Kingston at 7 pm.

The following three days were spent on the return journey to Oxford; this autumn weather was delightful and the river scenery magnificent; an insight into another way of life and indeed a memorable holiday.

Just north of Oxford is the vast Palladian building of Blenheim Palace which a grateful nation presented to the famous Duke of Marlborough after his successful campaign in the early 18th Century. The palace, situated in a magnificent park dominating the main street, was also the birthplace of Marlborough's illustrious descendant Sir Winston Churchill in 1874. It was built by the architect Vanbrugh and is open to the public.

PART

3

THE WEST COUNTRY

West of the inland port of Bristol, on the River Avon, is Bath, one of the leading spas in Britain, possessing the only hot springs in the country. Founded by the Romans as Aquae Sulis it contains many remains from that era, including the large colonnaded bath still in daily use, close by the Pump Room.

Its crescents and squares, which typify some of the finest existing examples of Georgian architecture, attracted all the leading figures of the 18th and 19th Centuries when Bath became a very fashionable venue.

The abbey, rebuilt in 1609, is of great interest and beauty in the ancient baths area and well known for its ecclesiastical music.

The Georgian houses in the Circus and the Royal Crescent are notable.

We spent time here in Bath whilst my stepmother was taking the treatment for arthritis.

Not far away, at the foot of the Mendip Hills, lies Wells which contains one of the smallest but most beautiful cathedrals in England. The west façade is the finest example of early English architecture, dating from 1190 to 1280.

The Bishop's Palace and the Vicar's Close, houses intended for the choirboys, are still in use. The white swans on the ancient moat ringing their dinner bell when hunger demands the attention of their keeper, are a charming sight.

Not far from Wells are the Wookey Hole Caves, a remarkable instance of stalagmites and stalactites developing over the ages, a forest of fantastic shapes. The Cheddar Gorge, winding between the limestone cliffs of the Mendip Hills, contains Gough's Caves, also remarkable natural caverns.

Glastonbury, a town of ancient myths and legends, witnessed the earliest beginning of Christianity in this country. Legend has it that St Joseph of Arimathea brought to it the Chalice of the Last Supper. On the Druidic Isle of Avalon he built a wooden church. On its site the ruins of a great abbey reputed to be the burial place of King Arthur and Queen Guinevere, still stand; in the abbey grounds, off-shoots of the Glastonbury Thorn, which sprang from St Joseph's staff, still grow luxuriantly and flower at Christmas time.

So in spite of industry and modern tourism, Glastonbury still retains the magic of bygone legend.

The Somerset coast facing the Bristol Channel, rocky, imposing and beautiful, contains several popular seaside resorts; Weston-Super-Mare, Burnham-on-Sea and Minehead, a centre for the Devon and Somerset staghounds which hunt the wild Exmoor country – the 'Lorna Doone' country.

Along the coast road we diverted to Burnham-on-Sea to visit friends and the church of St Andrew which contains an altar-piece designed by Inigo Jones and carried out by Grinling Gibbons.

About five miles from Bridgwater we found the delightful village of Westonzoyland situated in the marshlands of Sedgemoor where the ill-fated illegitimate son of Charles II was defeated in an unsuccessful bid for the throne of James II in 1685; it was the last battle to take place on English soil.

The villages of Chedzoy and Middlezoy on the island of Sowy (Zoy), two thousand acres of silt on the edge of Sedgemoor, form a unique area with three mediaeval churches of great architectural interest. We were told that these villages were originally colonized by refugees from Flanders who brought with them their skills in weaving, together with their Flemish names, but I have been unable to authenticate this claim.

At Westonzoyland we found a charming little hotel, built so close to the 'rhine' or canal that the windows looked down into the water; a very peaceful retreat for a few days.

Nearby is the island of Athelnay, surrounded in early times by marshes where King Alfred is reputed to have burnt the widow's cakes.

Yeovil is an attractive country town notable for glove making. Montacute, an exceptional Elizabethan mansion, is now the property of the National Trust.

Minehead is a popular watering place with a small harbour on the Bristol Channel. The restored Fisherman's Chapel dates from 1630 and there are old buildings and almshouses in the picturesque 'old village'.

The famous Missal De Sarum of Richard Fitzjames donated to the parish church of Minehead is a very rare example of mediaeval ecclesiastical office.

A curious hobby horse dance is a yearly May Day feature, probably an antique fertility rite.

The little village of Kitnor on Exmoor was inhabited by itinerant groups, including monks, for several hundred years, the first church being established in 635 AD.

About 1265 AD forty men were segregated in the village, banished as social outcasts for some forty years and thus it became a temporary jail for offenders,

85

criminals and undesirables. From 1544 the church and civil authorities peopled it as a leper colony and so it remained for seventy years.

Throughout these generations the little Norman church at Culbone, rebuilt four times, served as a focal point of existence; the smallest complete parish church in the country with a 14th Century screen, it is reached through dense woods from Porlock Weir.

In the late 1920s Dorothy Ball joined me in a trip to Devonshire and we found ourselves eventually in Lynmouth, a small seaside resort on the banks of the Lyn, backed by the wild expanse of Exmoor. In order to reach the quaint village of Lynton where we intended to stay it was necessary to take a steep mountain road which wound sinuously up the cliff.

Garage mechanics shook their heads over the small Austin 7 which in their opinion was far from adequate to undertake a journey which defeated much larger engines. 'It is too dangerous,' they said, 'a very narrow winding road of steep gradient and no emergency area.' But I was determined to go, thinking they were simply prejudiced against women drivers; after all it was only one mile!

The going was very tough. The rough road, down which hurtled large loose boulders, needed intense concentration. About half way up on an awkward bend the engine stopped and steam poured from the radiator. Fortunately, the brakes held long enough for me to place four big stones under the tyres and there we sat by the roadside watching the boiling radiator.

At last the thoughtful garage discovered that we had not made the journey and came to our rescue with emergency aid which helped us up to the top of the hill where a comfortable hotel awaited us.

☆ ☆ ☆

The old-world city of Salisbury in Wiltshire, in a green and pleasant valley, lies south of Warminster. Its beautiful cathedral has been the subject of many paintings by Constable and other artists, and the spire, rising to four hundred feet and reflected in the quiet waters of the River Avon which flows through the town, is reputed to be the tallest in England.

Grouped around the cathedral are the attractive houses of The Close, homes of the clergy and other notables; each is different in style, colour and size, creating a complete and somewhat remote entity; built from the 14th to the 18th Century.

Old Sarum, on the outskirts of the town, is a fortified hill occupied as a fortress by Romans, Saxons and Normans.

Wilton, once the capital of Wessex, is now widely known for the manufacture of carpets, and possesses a notable 18th Century Palladian bridge, spanning the River Nadder.

Not far from the town Wilton House, the palatial home of the Earls of Pembroke, contains Vandykes painted in situ, some of our greatest artistic treasures.

It is said that Shakespeare produced the first performance of *As You Like It* at Wilton House.

North of the town lies the rolling open expanse of Salisbury Plain, famous for the military training of many generations of armies.

The gigantic Druidic stone circle of Stonehenge is reputed to be four thousand years old, of which only a few stones remain. The even more ancient circle at Avebury is the most famous monument of antiquity in the British Isles. Nearby Savernake Forest, sixteen miles in circumference, is notable for its beech trees.

The charming town of Marlborough, known for its public school, contains many attractive old houses in the High Street.

Near Warminster is another magnificent Tudor house, Longleat, the property of the Marquis of Bath which is open to the public and contains a famous collection of pictures. It is now developed as a modern leisure centre.

☆　☆　☆

To the south lies the county of Dorset, an area of rich green meadows and rolling hills, particularly associated with Thomas Hardy's writings.

Its county town, Dorchester, the 'Casterbridge' of the novels, famous for the cruel assizes of the infamous Judge Jeffreys, contains a well-preserved Roman amphitheatre, Badbury Rings, some notable houses, fine churches and monuments and a 14th Century Easter Sepulchre. There is also the fascinating prehistoric fort of Maiden Castle, a vast neolithic camp of one hundred and fifteen acres dating from 3000 BC; here the Romans defeated the Celts in 44 AD and built a temple on the Celtic site.

From the picturesque village of Tolpuddle, workmen named the Tolpuddle Martyrs were tried and sentenced to transportation at Dorchester in 1834 for demanding a wage increase. Their protest was the foundation of the trade union movement.

Another interesting prehistoric camp overlooks the delightful little town of Blandford Forum from which a road leads northward to Shaftesbury where Benedictine nuns worshipped in the abbey founded by King Alfred in 880 AD.

On a beautiful bay to the east lies Poole, probably the

Poole, Dorset

oldest sea port on the south coast and a growing holiday resort. Round the ancient town are 15th Century almshouses, Scaplen's Court from the 14th or 15th Century, the Guildhall dating from 1761, the Customs House from the 18th Century and many other historic houses of similar dates which are now being restored.

Poole's prosperity was built upon the 18th Century trade with Newfoundland and recent archaeological excavations prove that the town was inhabited in mediaeval times by French, Italians and other European traders who made their headquarters there. It has recently become well known for the oil found beneath the harbour and this will add immeasurably to its future wealth and importance.

Marconi carried out successful wireless experiments with America from Sandbanks in 1898.

The largest natural harbour in the world at Poole attracts yachtsmen locally and from far afield. In it lies Brownsea Island with its restored castle and nature reserve, where Baden Powell instituted the Boy Scout movement.

On the Purbeck Hills, which form one bank of Poole Harbour, marble is quarried. The attractive seaside resort of Swanage nestling under Ballard Down contains many quaint houses and a forty ton block of Portland Stone carved into a globe. Nearby are the ruins of Corfe Castle, a 13th Century Norman building. King Edward the Martyr was murdered there by his mother in 978 AD. It was destroyed by Cromwell's army in 1646.

The village preserves old houses and inns, notably The Greyhound and the Bankes Arms.

Weymouth, a well known resort, was reputedly discovered by George III who lived at Gloucester House. A regular ferry service operating to the Channel Islands and France, has been extended to Spain.

Just along the coast from Weymouth is Portland, a narrow peninsula with an important naval harbour and breakwater to the north. To the west is Chesil Bank, a remarkable ridge extending from Portland to Abbotsbury composed of graduated pebbles, lying in an area of outstanding natural beauty. Portland Castle on Portland Bill was built by Henry VIII and the remains of Bow and Arrow Castle date from the 11th Century.

The famous Portland stone quarried here was used by Wren in the building of St Paul's Cathedral.

Bridport has celebrated its seven hundredth anniversary as a Royal Borough but its history extends much farther into the past. To the west lies Lyme Regis, one of the most attractive of Dorset's seaside resorts, standing almost in the sea, from which projects the stone breakwater known as The Cobb, where the Duke of Monmouth landed in 1685. There are a number of Georgian houses, almshouses of 1540 and an interesting perpendicular parish church. The thatched 'Umbrella Cottage' on the hill above The Cobb is attractive and there are links with Jane Austen's novel *Persuasion*.

There are still many lovely and unspoilt villages in Dorset, at present quite untouched by tourism and west of Lyme Regis there are a number of charming holiday resorts on the coast of Devonshire.

SOUTH WEST ENGLAND

Sidmouth and Budleigh Salterton are two lovely small resorts near the mouth of the River Sid, and I have spent many happy holidays in both villages. At the former I used to stay at an hotel on the promenade, my bedroom overlooking the local cricket ground so that I could rest in bed, lulled by the crack of bat on ball.

In September 1939, I was on holiday in Sidmouth with my foster father and his wife in lovely weather and we were enjoying the companionship of a high-ranking military officer and his family. One evening after dinner he remarked, 'I am on emergency recall at any time and I think I should say goodbye to you tonight in case I don't see you again.'

So we said farewell and, the next morning he had gone.

This alerted us to the possibility that war was imminent, so we started home next day. Although it was Sunday we were surprised and puzzled to see gangs of men painting white lines along the main roads to the north, but in the years of blackout which ensued we were very grateful for Hore Belisha's foresight.

War with Germany was declared that day.

The charming hotel at Budleigh Salterton, now demolished, was built on the shingle beach, quite unspoilt at that time: it was a haven of peace. The small village has now become a favourite retirement area.

My foster mother was very fond of Exmouth, but I consider it has scant claim to beauty except for the rather attractive little harbour with its fishing fleet. There are a few Georgian houses and only two miles away is La Ronde, an octagonal 18th Century twelve-sided building, housing the unique Parminster Collection of Curiosities.

Exeter, the county town of Devonshire, picturesquely situated on the River Exe, is a university city. There are many interesting architectural features in the beautiful cathedral built between 1260 and 1380. It is a fine example of the decorated style and there are several old churches in the city. The Guildhall dates from 1330, Wynard's Hospital was founded in 1436 and St Nicholas' Priory is an interesting Tudor building.

Part of Rougemont Castle, erected by William the Conqueror, has survived and in its grounds are the remains of the ancient city walls containing many fine Georgian and Regency houses and terraces.

About fourteen miles south of Exeter lies Teignmouth, a charming little seaside town, whilst still further south is Torquay, which claims to have the mildest climate in England, and is notable as a yachting centre with every possible tourist facility. Close to the seafront is the historic Spanish Barn in which four hundred prisoners from a galleon of the Spanish Armada were imprisoned in 1588.

Buckfast Abbey, founded in the 10th Century and refounded two centuries later, has been restored by the monks themselves at the present day as their home.

There are many delightful villages not far away including Cockington, a living picture of mediaeval England, and Paignton, a holiday resort in the sweep of Torbay whose municipal offices are now housed in the

93

Clovelly

beautiful mansion of Oldway, once used as an American hospital.

Brixham is a notable fishing village at which William of Orange disembarked in 1688 on his way to assume the throne of England. South of Brixham on the River Dart is Dartmouth, guarded by its castle built by Henry VIII. It is also of note for its famous naval college and one of its greatest attractions is the steamer trip up the River Dart to Totnes, a village with a history of a thousand years, dominated by the remains of a Norman castle and many interesting Elizabethan houses.

Kingsbridge, a picturesque little town convenient for excursions along the Devonshire coast, lies at the head of the River Salcombe, whilst the coastal village of that name is famous as a yachting centre.

The attractive yachting centre, beautifully situated at the mouth of the Kingsbridge estuary, possesses a picturesque harbour. It is linked to East Portsmouth by a passenger ferry.

Plymouth, farther to the west, with its neighbour Devonport, ranks second only to Portsmouth as a naval base and dockyard. Plymouth Hoe, an excellent outlook for shipping, is best known for the game of bowls which Sir Francis Drake completed before his fight with the Spanish Armada which was then sailing up the Channel.

In September 1620, the small ship *Mayflower* of one hundred and eighty tons left to carry the Pilgrim Fathers to the New World, past Smeaton Tower, the old Eddystone lighthouse.

Much of the city centre, with St Andrew's Church, was damaged by bombs and has been rebuilt, together with Mount Edgecumbe (16th to 18th Century) in its lovely grounds.

The famous Antarctic explorer Captain Scott was born in Plymouth in 1868.

One of the best views of the city is from the high railway at the rear of the town.

☆ ☆ ☆

Cornwall, a most unusual county, a long peninsula narrowing to the toe and bounded on both sides by the sea, offers a wide choice of seaside resorts situated in colourful scenery. It is the warmest area in England.

The inland scenery, however, is somewhat uninteresting, with its mines and excavations.

The two charming villages of East and West Looe are linked by a modern bridge spanning the River Looe. On my first trip in 1919, it was only accessible by single track railway and waggonette from Liskeard.

West Looe Church has a campanile and the quaint streets and ancient inns are a delight to the visitor; a pillory has been preserved outside the 10th Century Guildhall.

Tourism and fishing are the main occupations and shark fishing on a large scale has recently become popular.

Fowey is a delightful little town with buildings dating from Tudor times. Farther along the coast, Falmouth is sheltered in a fine natural harbour which winds among beechwoods and sub-tropical plants. It contains some quaint narrow streets and the interesting 17th Century church of King Charles the Martyr.

The 16th Century Pendennis Castle is an excellent viewpoint.

Truro, one of the more interesting towns of inland Cornwall, is chiefly notable for its lovely modern cathedral partly built over the old parish church: its spire reaches to two hundred and forty feet and important features are a carved stone reredos and a beautiful baptistry.

In Helston, an ancient town with many interesting features, the curious Floral or Furry Dance, held usually on the 8th May, takes place in the streets; its origin is unknown.

In Mount's Bay lies Penzance, capital of the Cornish Riviera. Nearby is St Michael's Mount, an ancient 14th Century castle set on a rock which at high tide becomes an island. Here Perkin Warbeck proclaimed himself King in 1493. The restaurant built in the castle was once famous for its omelettes which I enjoyed on my first visit.

Land's End, the westernmost point of the English coast, with granite cliffs six hundred feet high, has recently been developed into a leisure area, although it is listed as an area of outstanding natural beauty.

Newquay, one of my favourite resorts, is constantly buffeted by the fierce Atlantic gales. It is divided across several small bays, each with its own fine beach and all well known for bathing and surfing.

At the close of World War II, Hilda and I set out to take a holiday in a country house near Newquay which had been occupied during the war by the boys of a public school.

The fine building stood on a promontory in a beautiful setting by the sea, but had been severely damaged by the schoolboys.

The devastation was appalling: priceless paintings on the walls had been used as dartboards, entirely destroying their value; large holes bored into the skirting boards allowed easy access from room to room and the interior walls were covered with graffiti.

Although full to capacity with visitors, it was a most unsuitable holiday venue.

St Michael's Mount

But the unsatisfactory state of our accommodation was not the only problem; the new manager had arrived on the previous day to find an inexperienced, incompetent staff with the result that the domestic arrangements were in chaos. After several late and inedible meals, the guests met together to discuss our grievances. There is no better way to know one's fellow travellers.

Finally we enlisted the help of the local council and, as a short-term solution, we agreed to provide and cook the meals ourselves, until new staff could be recruited.

But slowly the guests drifted away and so did we.

Farther north is Tintagel, in rather a gloomy setting of rocky and wild scenery, reputed to be the birthplace of King Arthur. Like Bude, it is very popular with tourists.

The wild desolate stretch of Dartmoor lies across the county north to south from Bude to Torquay and this can best be visited from Okehampton whose history, with its Iron Age fort, dates back to before Saxon and Roman times.

This extensive upland expanse is now a national park which conserves areas of great beauty and unusual wildlife. Prehistoric remains, ancient crosses and stone circles testify to early habitations.

SOUTH ENGLAND

The well known resort of Bournemouth situated amongst gardens and pine trees is noted for its picturesque chines, the Russell Côtes Art Gallery and the East Cliff rock gardens. It has also established a high reputation for first class concerts by the Bournemouth Symphony Orchestra.

Lying between the River Avon and Southampton Water is the protected area of the New Forest and amongst the beautiful woodland roads and paths can be seen the native breed of wild pony and small herds of deer.

The forest, enlarged by William the Conqueror as a hunting reserve, now comprises about one hundred and forty square miles owned partly by the Crown, the forest laws being administered by verderers from their courts at Lyndhurst. King William II (Rufus) was killed near Minstead in 1100 AD.

On the Beaulieu River are the remains of the 13th Century abbey, part of which is now the parish church. In the nearby motor museum are displayed more than two hundred veteran and vintage cars and cycles in the Palace House, the home of Lord Montagu.

Close to the town at the edge of the New Forest lies Buckler's Hard. Wooden warships were built here, notably Nelson's *Agamemnon* in 1781 which was then towed to Plymouth for fitting out.

Romsey is an attractive country town, famous for its abbey, dating back to the 10th Century and containing many notable features.

Broadlands, a massive 18th Century house in the Palladian style, is situated in a fine park near Romsey and here Queen Elizabeth II and later Prince Charles spent their honeymoons.

Farther west is Southampton, an important modern transatlantic port with extensive docks. King Henry V marshalled his army here, prior to the victory of Agincourt in 1414 and the West Quay was the scene of the *Mayflower's* sailing with the Pilgrim Fathers on the first stage of their journey to America in 1620: this is recorded by the tall Pilgrim Fathers' memorial.

Although Southampton was heavily bombed in the war, there still remain many interesting features: ancient walls with their towers, a Norman house called Canute's Palace, important churches and many other buildings from early times.

A car ferry connects with the Isle of Wight from the entrance of Southampton Water.

THE ISLE OF WIGHT

The Isle of Wight, famous as a yachting centre, consists of an area of about a hundred and fifty square miles and boasts a number of popular holiday resorts: Ryde, Bembridge, Sandown, Shanklin and Ventnor on the east coast, all displaying picturesque coastal scenery. Cowes is the headquarters of yachting in the British Isles, the home of the Royal Yacht Squadron and the centre for many regattas.

Among the famous people associated with the island is

Queen Victoria who died at her home, Osborne House, in 1901. The poets Lord Tennyson and Swinburne were residents on the island.

Charles I was imprisoned in Carisbrooke Castle near Newport and amongst other attractions are the Roman villa at Brading, the well known chalk cliffs known as The Needles, standing in the sea off the westernmost point, and the coloured sands of Alum Bay.

Much of the island is registered as an area of outstanding natural beauty.

CHANNEL ISLANDS

The four Channel Islands, lying about fifty miles from the English coast, are well known for their beautiful scenery, mild climate and the various breeds of cattle. St Helier is the capital of Jersey, dominated by the massive Elizabethan Castle. St Peter Port, capital of Guernsey, is the centre for many interesting excursions round the islands.

Both Alderney and Sark suffered very much from the German occupation of World War II; the former is famous for its bird sanctuaries, whilst Sark is content to live in a past age under the feudal rule of its Seigneur, who controls all modern progress.

Fareham is an old market town and port at the head of a small creek on Southampton Water, the childhood home of Thackeray.

It was in the autumn of 1938 that Mary Sarjant and I set out in my Austin 7 for a short holiday and, after a few days in the Cotswolds at Evesham, we travelled south,

102

arriving at Fareham in the late afternoon, where the review of the fleet by the King and Queen was scheduled for the following day.

Not having reserved in advance, we found it almost impossible to obtain suitable accommodation but, after many attempts, an enquiry in a local shop prompted a resident to offer us rooms in her house.

At the evening meal we met her son, an airman on duty at the Naval Review, who advised us where to go for a good sight of the proceedings and gave me tickets and a car sticker.

Next morning we set off to follow his instructions and showing the tickets at some large and imposing gates, we were surprised to be saluted without question, as we were ushered through to a parking space near the main marquee.

It all seemed very easy. We showed the tickets again and made our way into a huge luncheon tent where we were directed to two seats and, to our astonishment on looking round, we saw the Royal Party having lunch at the far end of the marquee.

Frankly I was terrified, for we were only dressed in holiday clothes, entirely out of place in such a scenario.

However, there it was, so we hastened to consume the very delicious buffet lunch as soon as possible and to make our escape outside to see the review.

The spectacle of our naval might was pathetic; a small number of ships, two submarines and a flight past of half a dozen sea planes, scarcely indicating adequate preparation for the holocaust which was to take place so soon afterwards.

Returning to our lodging, we met again the young man who had arranged such an enjoyable day for us: he knew quite well where we had been!

Portsmouth, the largest of the Royal Navy's dockyards covering three hundred acres, contains many 18th Century buildings. Here is berthed on dry land, Lord Nelson's famous flagship *HMS Victory,* launched in 1765. Southsea, a near neighbour and a pleasant holiday resort commands fine views of the Isle of Wight and the shipping in Spithead.

Bomb damage during World War II was severe but there are many historical houses and churches now restored which are of great interest. Charles Dickens, George Meredith and Brunel were born in Portsmouth.

A few miles inland is Winchester, a former Roman centre, the ancient capital of England, one of the most historical and beautiful cities in the country. In its splendid mediaeval cathedral are buried William II (Rufus), who was killed whilst hunting in the New Forest, Izaak Walton, author of the *Compleat Angler*, St Swithin, Bishop of Winchester, and Jane Austen.

In Winchester Castle is King Arthur's Round Table and by the River Itchen is the college founded by William Wykeham in 1382, the oldest public school in England. The Hospital of St Cross, dedicated in 1136 for the care of 'thirteen poor brethren', is a superbly beautiful building and still dispenses largesse to the poor.

One of the many picturesque villages in the surrounding country is Chawton, Jane Austen's home, and Selborne immortalized by Gilbert White in his *Natural History.*

☆ ☆ ☆

Across the borders of Hampshire to the east is the lovely area known as the Highlands of Surrey of which

104

Hindhead is a prominent feature. The picturesque town of Haslemere is well known for the Dolmetsch Festival held each year, where baroque music is played on facsimiles of the original instruments.

The attractive market town of Farnham boasts many historical houses and inns, and Farnham Castle of the 12th Century with a fine 16th Century tower, now a college, was formerly the residence of the Bishops of Guildford. It is of great interest to me, as my foster parents are both buried there in the old churchyard.

Guildford, the county town of Surrey, is situated amidst some of the finest scenery in England. Mentioned in the will of Alfred the Great (871-901) there is evidence of its past history in the many ancient and picturesque buildings which line the steeply climbing High Street. Not far away are several great houses containing notable treasures of interest.

Chichester in Sussex is a cathedral city, known to the Romans as Regium. Its old city walls still survive and the fine early Norman cathedral combines several styles of architecture. St Mary's Hospital, a Tudor almshouse, is an interesting feature of this delightful area. Not far away, on the property of the Duke of Richmond, is Goodwood Racecourse, where each July is held one of the most fashionable meetings of the season.

At Arundel, the imposing Norman castle, home of the Dukes of Norfolk, stands on a hill dominating the town, a landmark seen for miles. There are several interesting churches and other buildings, dating from the 14th Century.

Pulborough, a pleasant town in which to spend a weekend contains several old houses and an early

English church with a massive 12th Century font and a charming 14th Century lychgate.

At Fishbourne, a large Roman palace has been partially excavated, but a main motor highway has been constructed during the centuries, precluding further discoveries.

On the coast to the south lies the pleasant holiday resort of Bognor Regis, so-called from King George V who convalesced there in 1929. Together with Littlehampton and Worthing, all have still retained the peaceful atmosphere of the Sussex countryside. Having friends near Littlehampton, I have been privileged to explore this district very thoroughly.

A few miles away on the South Downs, at Glyndebourne, is a small manor house, partly Tudor, which has a modern opera house in the extensive grounds. Here is produced a varied programme of opera during the summer season to which we made an annual pilgrimage for some years, staying at Lewes or Alfriston on each visit for several nights.

One of life's supreme pleasures is to visit the Glyndebourne complex, arriving on a summer's afternoon for tea on the lawn of the lovely gardens. Later to tour the interesting manor house, often to the accompaniment of a rehearsal in a neighbouring room, to observe the cosmopolitan audience of royalties, politicians, musicians and artists of every race and colour and to watch the many young people seek a suitable site for their picnic dinner party later.

After enjoying the first half of the scheduled opera we partook of a superb dinner provided during the long interval and when the curtain had fallen on the last act, the drive to the ancient inn on a starlit night concluded a magical day.

Brighton, the undisputed prince of seaside resorts, has

a special charm, probably engendered by its elegant Regency setting, much of which remains undisturbed. The spectacular Pavilion in the town centre, by the great decorative artist Nash in the oriental style, testifies to the Hanoverian revelry of his day – whilst the royal stables have been converted into a spacious concert hall. Some denigrate the town as tawdry and superficial but for me it still retains the grandeur of its past.

Almost the continuation of Brighton is Hove, where Regency architecture is seen at its most dignified and most charming.

East Grinstead, not far away, rich in 17th Century timbered houses is surrounded by beautiful wooded countryside in which there are many picturesque villages. It is famous for its special hospital dealing with war casualties.

Midway between Tunbridge Wells and Hastings, lies the lovely 14th Century moated castle of Bodiam, now in ruins. Closer to the coast is Herstmonceux with a 15th Century red brick castle. Pevensey Castle, a sombre ruin dating back to the time of the Romans, Saxons and Normans is not far from Eastbourne, a resort well known for the imposing white cliffs of Beachy Head, with its fine marine views.

Hastings, a very progressive seaside town, has a high reputation by reason of its annual music festival and is a popular centre for international conferences. After the Battle of Hastings in 1066, William the Conqueror built an abbey to commemorate his victory, and its neighbour, Bexhill-on-Sea, has an interesting church dating from 1070.

Inland, Kent has many interesting places; Tunbridge

Sissinghurst, Kent

Wells, a fashionable 18th Century town recorded by Thackeray and Meredith, forms a good centre. Its chief feature is The Pantiles, a colonnaded row of shops of great architectural charm.

The Cinque Ports – Dover, Hastings, Romney, Hythe and Sandwich – were so named in the reign of Edward the Confessor and, in return for certain privileges, they furnished ships for the protection of the coast. In Sandwich, a charming little old-world town, almost every house seems to belong to a fairy story and at Walmer Castle near Deal, Julius Caesar made his first landing in 55 BC.

Dover, chief of the Cinque Ports, is a town of great interest. On the hills overlooking the busy harbour and cross-channel port stands a Norman castle in the grounds of which is the oldest building in England, the two thousand-year-old Pharos, the lighthouse which guided the Roman supply ships into the harbour.

The famous Shakespeare Cliff part of the 'white cliffs' of Dover is graphically described in *King Lear*.

Folkestone, a popular holiday resort, is sheltered by its position at the foot of chalk cliffs and contains the remains of Roman buildings. The Leas, extensive gardens fronting the sea, form a well known promenade, of great beauty.

The sea has long since receded from Hythe, but it possesses two curiosities, the early English church, beneath which is a collection of hundreds of human skulls and the miniature railway, the smallest in the world, which runs along the coast to Dymchurch on the edge of Romney Marsh and Dungeness. My visit during the war was frequently interrupted by air raids.

Early in the 1950s one of my friends in Winchelsea invited me as the principal guest to present the prizes on speech day at her school and so I travelled down to keep the appointment, staying overnight at the school.

It so happened that one of her clients was an ex-pupil of mine and on the following day, she took me to her home in Rye, a miniature fortified town of great beauty overlooking the Romney Marshes. Here I spent an exciting weekend exploring the Norman perpendicular church and the quaint winding streets with their fascinating dwellings. The American novelist, Henry James, lived in an 18th Century house here for some years and both Thackeray and Dickens had associations here.

A few miles inland is Canterbury, one of the most beautiful of all English cities: a Roman town, it has thirteen hundred years of continuous history and saw the beginnings of Christianity in England as preached by St Augustine in the year 597 AD. For centuries it has been the archipiscopal see of the Primate and in 1170 the saintly archbishop Thomas à Becket was murdered there. Between the south piers is the tomb of the Black Prince above which hang his helmet, shield and surcoat.

Apart from the lovely 11th to 15th Century cathedral there are many ancient churches, houses and inns of great historical interest and fortunately the intensive bombing of the world wars did not destroy them.

The King's School, one of the oldest in England, has a unique exterior Norman staircase.

On the coast are many seaside resorts. Herne Bay has seven miles of seafront and near the Roman remains of Reculver are Whitstable, famous for its oysters, Margate, Broadstairs and Ramsgate.

The ancient city of Rochester at the mouth of the River Medway within thirty miles of London, is dominated by the fine Norman castle and a cathedral built upon the foundations of a Saxon church, dating from 604 AD.

Dickens, the great novelist, lived nearby on Gads Hill and at Cobham Hall, five miles away, La Belle Stuart spent her honeymoon as the Duchess of Richmond.

The remains of ancient buildings in the town are of considerable interest.

THE LONDON AREA

Within the immediate neighbourhood of the city of London are some of the most beautiful and historic places in England and of these Windsor Castle is probably first. It was William the Conqueror who changed Windsor Castle from a Saxon hunting lodge into a Norman military post and finally into a royal residence which became the home of English Kings for nine hundred years.

The castle stands upon a hill overlooking the River Thames, huge, dignified and permanent.

Many royals have added to its splendour through the intervening centuries: there is a superb collection of pictures, particularly those of Vandyke, a magnificent library, much fine armour and many other artistic and historical treasures including the famous collection of Holbein crayon studies of prominent people in the reign of Henry VIII.

St George's Chapel, built by Edward IV (1461-1483), one of the finest Perpendicular buildings in England contains beautiful fan vaulting, and the coffins of many English Kings, including Henry VIII and Charles I. King George VI is buried there. One of my young pupils won a scholarship to the choir school and another was married in this lovely chapel.

The town of Windsor, attractive and typically English,

is linked by a bridge to the other bank of the Thames to Eton College, the most famous public school in England. It was founded in 1440 by Henry VI whose stately stone-built chapel fills one side of School Yard, in contrast to the red brick buildings of Lupton Tower and Upper and Lower Schools dating from the 15th to the 17th Centuries. The library preserves the original of Gray's *Elegy* amongst its manuscripts and the well known playing fields stretch towards the River Thames. Very many famous names are associated with the school.

In the Home Park is Frogmore Mausoleum in which Queen Victoria and Prince Albert are buried. Windsor Great Park covers about two thousand acres which are beautifully wooded and traversed by public roads. About forty-five acres are now a Forest Reserve.

A short distance from Eton is the pretty village of Stoke Poges, the scene of Gray's famous *Elegy* and close by is the tract of forest known as Burnham Beeches. In the little village of Chalfont-St-Giles is preserved the cottage to which Milton returned in 1665, during the Great Plague of London to write *Paradise Lost* and *Paradise Regained.*

In the Thames Valley, close to the town of Egham, is the historic island where in 1215 King John was forced by his barons to grant Magna Carta, the first declaration of the citizen's rights. Not far from Egham is Virginia Water, a picturesque lake created in 1746, fringed with magnificent trees on the edge of Windsor Great Park.

Maidenhead, a gay river resort, caters for the boating fraternity and not far away is Cliveden House, the historic home of Viscount Astor, now the property of the National Trust.

Twenty miles north of London lies St Albans, the ancient town named after the first Christian martyr in England; a Roman soldier, beheaded for his faith in 303 AD. The cathedral, possessing the longest nave of any mediaeval church, contains relics of Roman and Saxon masonry in its structure including an amphitheatre.

At the Battle of St Albans in 1455, Henry VI was captured by the Yorkists. On the outskirts of the town are the remains of the Roman town of Verulamum founded in 43 AD, possessing the only Roman theatre discovered in England.

Hatfield House, the magnificent home of the Marquis of Salisbury, is one of the finest Tudor houses in existence: Queen Elizabeth I as princess was confined at Hatfield by her sister, Mary Tudor.

Epping Forest, a stretch of woodland eleven miles long, was once part of the royal hunting forest of Waltham, the site of the abbey founded by Harold, the last of the Saxon kings: the forest is now the home of foxes, badgers and red deer.

South of London, Kingston-upon-Thames, the first place above London Bridge where the River Thames is easily crossed, saw much fighting during the Civil War. In front of the town hall is the ancient Coronation Stone upon which seven Saxon Kings were probably crowned, Edward the Elder, the last one, in 900 AD.

Near Kingston is Hampton Court, the beautiful red brick palace built by Cardinal Wolsey and taken from him by Henry VIII. It is said to be haunted by the ghosts of Jane Seymour and Catherine Howard; its gardens are magnificent, especially in spring when the fruit trees and flowering shrubs are in bloom.

Not far away is Ham House, dating from 1610, the home of the Duke of Lauderdale, a member of Charles II's Cabal Ministry, 1668-1673. The house contains a fine collection of restoration furniture and behind it stretches a large expanse of Richmond Park which Charles I enclosed as a playground for his children.

Within the park is White Lodge, a large Palladian house built by George II and occupied by most of the Kings and Queens of England since then.

The town of Richmond commands a famous view of the Thames which has stimulated many artists, but only a gateway of the old Palace of Richmond now remains; it was a favourite residence of the rulers of England and here in 1603 died Queen Elizabeth I.

It is almost impossible to list all the places of interest around London and within the city itself, for every corner of this area is steeped in history.

For nearly thirty years I travelled once a month up to the capital for meetings and yet managed to see only a fraction of these wonders.